It's the Little Things That Count

IT'S THE LITTLE THINGS THAT COUNT

RICHARD PATTERSON, JR.

THOMAS NELSON PUBLISHERS
Nashville

Library of Congress Cataloging-in-Publication Data

Patterson, Richard, 1948-

    It's the little things that count / Richard Patterson, Jr.

       p.   cm.

    Includes bibliographical references.

    ISBN 0-8407-6243-7

    1. Parents—Untited States—Time management. 2. Parenting—United States. 3. Family—United States. 4. Family—United States—Religious life. 5. Marriage—United States. I. Title.

HQ755.8.P398   1993

306.87—dc20   93-13298

                                              CIP

Printed in the United States of America.

1 2 3 4 5 6 7   97 96 95 94 93

DEDICATION

To my wife, Sara, and my sons, Jeremy and Zachary. There are no greater rewards than spending time and being family with them.

"*Dost Thou Love Life? Then do not Squander Time: for that is the stuff life is made of.*"

Benjamin Franklin

"*Be very careful, then, how you live—not as unwise but as wise, making the most of every opportunity...*"

St. Paul (Ephesians 5: 15-16)

CONTENTS

Introduction: Unlocking the Secret

It was one of my favorite television shows when I was a child. The contestants had to complete some funny task while a big studio clock ticked off the seconds. If they finished before time ran out, they "beat the clock" and won a prize. If time ran out before they had a chance to reach their goal, the clock "beat" them.

The show was called "Beat the Clock." I was reminded of it while thinking about what life is like for many families today: single-parent families, two-career families, families with only one parent working outside the home—in fact, most families. Life gets pretty hectic for all of us.

My schedule includes a fair amount of traveling and work on nights and weekends. My wife has a full-time career as a public school teacher. Almost daily we wrestle with how to find enough time to spend with each other and our two sons.

You may have read the same statistics I have: parents today spend 40 percent less time with their children than parents did in 1965.[1] Spouses, too, are spending less time together.[2]

Is this true? I don't know. But I do know this: it doesn't have to be true of either my family or yours. Sure, we are pressured from all sides. We have heavy responsibilities as parents and spouses. But if our goal is to have enough time to really enjoy our families, I'm convinced we can "beat the clock."

"Beating the clock" means at least two things. First, it means *maximizing the time we already spend with our families*. Second, it means identifying the activities that mean the most to family life and investing our limited time in them. Investors know that you don't have to start with large amounts of capital to accumulate wealth. Careful, regular investment of small amounts over a long period of time is what builds a fortune. Likewise, regular, small investments of time are the secret to "beating the clock" in family life.

So, in the pages that follow we'll focus our attention on these two areas: making the most of the time we already have with our families and selecting the most important activities in which to invest our limited time with them. First, however, we'll need to spend a few pages understanding what we're up against—the pressures of our busy lifestyles and how they weigh on our marriage and family relationships. It's important to know our enemy before we go into battle.

Encouraged and Equipped

As we do, we'll discuss some hard, maybe even unpleasant situations of choices every now and then. We need to look at them head on. Then we can discover how to overcome them. When we do discuss hard situations, remember that the purpose is not to make anyone feel guilty. We're all on this journey together. The important thing is that you come away from our journey encouraged and equipped to reach your goal of really enjoying your family!

In chapter 2, you may be surprised to discover that there are many times already "built in" to your daily schedule which you can use to strengthen your family. Some of these are very "special times" which you can use to "make the most of what we've (already) got" to enjoy your family.

Few of us parents today can be with our children at any and all times of the day. For many of us-especially single parents-it's a struggle to be with them as much as we'd like. But even when we can't be with them, we can often be available to them. Single mothers are really pioneering in this area. We'll meet some of them in chapter 3.

Next we'll share the secrets of some folks who've built strong, lasting marriages. They face a daily contest with the clock, too. But with the help of some of the daily disciplines, they've discovered some effective ways-big and small- to use their limited time together to strengthen their marriages.

Apart from worship and faith-building activities, nothing is more important than establishing and maintaining family rituals and traditions. We'll "look over the shoulder" of both single-parent and two-parent families to see how they strengthen and enjoy their families in this way.

We'll also devote some time to discussing how family fun is serious business! And we'll take a detailed look at how businesses and corporations are helping working parents to spend more time with their children.

At the end of each chapter, you'll find a few questions or other exercises. Their purpose is to help you put into practice right away some of the suggestions and principles about which you'll be reading. That way you won't waste time getting started at "beating the clock"!

Ultimately, "beating the clock" to enjoy our families takes more than just a time management approach. It requires a spiritual approach also. Underlying all that is written here is a commitment to the truth of the Christian faith and to the Lord of that faith—Jesus Christ.

Nevertheless, to nurture your family's faith requires a struggle with the clock. Even if more traditional means, such as family devotions, have fallen along the wayside, you needn't give up altogether. We'll look at some alternative strategies for nurturing family faith.

A weekly family "Sabbath" of rest, recreation, and worship is essential to reaching that goal. A visit to your local shopping mall on Sunday morning will attest to the fact that many people don't feel that a family sabbath is worth much. But believe me, it gives much more than it takes. It helps create what the Greeks called *kairos*, that "time outside of time," a renewing, refreshing, redeeming time that families caught up in the battle with the clock so desperately want and need.

Every day brings our families new opportunities to be together, to enjoy each other, and to grow together in love and faith. How will we use those opportunities? These ancient words are still full of wisdom today: "Be careful, then, how you live—not as unwise, but as wise, making the most of every opportunity."[3]

That's the secret to beating the clock and really enjoying our families. And that's the secret we're ready to unlock together now.

PART ONE

Winning the Daily Battles

CHAPTER ONE

_____

_____

_____

Beating the Clock:
Meeting the Challenge,
Building Our Confidence

My eight-year-old son had to be at his Little League game at 6:00 P.M. My wife's grad school course (which met twice weekly) started at the same time. My teenage son had his mid-week youth meeting at church at 6:30. I was glad all I had to do was be the family "chauffeur."

We hardly had time to wave to each other as we went in and out of the house and car that evening. For us to have dinner together would have required the planning and scheduling capabilities of a mainframe computer.

The Pennsylvania Dutch have an apt expression for how I felt that day: "The hurrier I go, the behinder I get." Maybe your family has had a few days like that, too.

Beating the clock to find time to enjoy our families is a daily challenge. However, we *can* meet the challenge. I'm convinced of that. But first it helps to "scout out the enemy" and understand the nature of the challenge so that we can see the way to success.

The Shortcut Society

Time magazine has called America the "Shortcut Society."[1] We are committed to saving time at all costs. One particularly telling example of our mania for hurrying and saving time is that of the lady who paid two young entrepreneurs $20 to deliver $.59 worth of hot dog buns to a family picnic because she didn't have time to do it herself! Those young businessmen charge $25-50 per hour to do just about anything: return your videotapes, fix a broken light socket, or even deliver your hot dog buns—all in the interest of helping you save time.[2]

Saving time is a goal many people pursue today as zealously as they do making money or achieving success. All kinds of time- and labor-saving devices, from microwave ovens to fax machines, have become a permanent part of our lives. You'd think we would be awash in "free time." Ironically, the opposite is true.

Louis Harris, whose polls and surveys chronicle the American lifestyle, reports that the actual amount of leisure time enjoyed by the average American has *decreased* by 37 percent since 1973. Over that same period, the average work week has increased by nearly 20 percent.[3] Despite all of our shortcuts, we are saving less time than ever.

We feel this time shrinkage in our families, also. Dolores Curran, in her helpful study, *Stress and the Healthy Family*, cites a poll of over one thousand working parents that revealed "63% of working mothers and 40% of working fathers said they didn't have enough time for themselves. The same survey revealed that 26% felt a lack of time with their children and with each other."[4]

Curran observes that "practically every study of family stress puts time pressures near the top." She points out that four of the top ten stresses on families today deal directly with time pressures: not enough time together as a couple, not enough family fun time, not enough "me" time, and an overscheduled family calendar.[5]

It seems that the Pennsylvania Dutch were right. With all of our hurrying to save time, we still don't have enough to just enjoy being a family. This is frustrating, but it's also a challenge that we can meet.

Time Together As Spouses

Two psychologists posed this question in a magazine article for parents: "If you were given $10,000 and told to do something nice for your children, how would you spend it?"[6] Would you take your children on a trip to Disney World or, perhaps, to Europe? (Europe was my first response.) Perhaps you'd set up a college fund for their education. Or buy them a backyard pool so they could have summer swim parties with their friends (at least it would keep them home!).

A better idea, suggest the psychologists, might be to send you and your spouse on a trip to Hawaii!

But weren't we told to do something nice for the children?

What does a vacation for the parents do for *them*? The answer lies in the direct relationship between the quality of your marriage and the health and happiness of your children.

It's probably no coincidence that the divorce rate has accelerated rapidly at the same time that the daily contest with the clock has kept many couples from having time to be together and enjoy each other.[7]

One family counselor put it this way: "It is the marriage that made the child and it is the marriage that grows the child."[8] The relationship between the adults sets the tone for all family relationships. "It's a simple statement of how people live in the system we call a family. Parents set the tone for the entire family process."[9]

The stronger and healthier the parental relationship, the more positive will be their relationship with their children and the healthier will be the overall environment in the home. Family life will be more enjoyable in this kind of home, too. So you needn't always feel guilty about that evening out, a weekend away without the children, or even a vacation without them. It might be time well spent for your entire family.

But what if you're a single parent?

Tired Is My Middle Name

Single-parent families are on the increase today and they face special challenges from the clock, also. The great majority of single parents are mothers. Since over half of all single mothers work outside the home to help support the family, many feel the pressures of time in an even greater way than parents with partners.

"You have full-time work and then you come home and work," said one divorced mother in New York. "You have to do everything yourself. You have to know everything your kids are up to. If there's an accident, all the responsibility is yours."[10]

When these single mothers get home from work at night, there's no other adult to help with the dinner, or clean up after the meal, or put the children to bed while they do the laundry or just relax.

When the children need to go to a doctor's appointment, there's no spouse to say "I'll do it." After-school activities can make a single parent feel like she lives in the car. Weekends can be tough, too. Just when there ought to be some "me" time, the children need transportation halfway across town.

Financial pressures never seem to let up, either. A single-parent family (one in five families with young children are single-parent families) has a fifty-fifty chance of living below the poverty line.[11] In California, for example, the effect of the average divorce is to decrease the standard of living of a woman and her minor children by 73 percent.[12]

One single mother who works two jobs is typical of the plight of many. She works days as a medical technician and four nights a week as a waitress. "Tired is my middle name," she says. "I'm exhausted all the time."[13]

I know many single mothers (and you probably do, too) who are beating the clock every day and finding creative ways to be with and enjoy their families. We're going to meet some of these parents in just about every chapter to come.

The Biggest "Time Gobbler"

Of all the forces that rob families of time together, the biggest culprit is work. For most of us, our jobs are the single biggest time commitment of our day. Both our family's survival and our own self-esteem are tied closely to our work.

However, our work is often at odds with our families. The unspoken values of the workplace have long dictated that commitment to one's job take priority over one's family. Men, who for centuries dominated the marketplace, were in turn dominated by these values (what I have called "careerism" elsewhere).[14]

Although there are signs of change, it is still true that many employers expect work to take precedence over family schedules.[15] In many companies, the way to prove your commitment to your job (and to get ahead) is to work long hours and most weekends or to spend much of each work week "on the road" away from home and family.

The rapid increase in two-career families has greatly magnified the time pressures on families. In the case of over half of two-parent families today, both parents work outside the home to some extent. These parents often feel as though there's just not enough time to go around. My two-career family certainly feels it. Maybe yours does, too.

Yale Psychologist Edward Ziglar warns that American society is "at the breaking point as far as family [time] is concerned." Now, "even parents who like their jobs and love their kids find the pressure to do justice to both becomes almost unbearable."[16]

For example, nearly one-third of all families in this country do not eat dinner together, and over 40 percent do not eat breakfast together, either. Yet, mealtime is the one time of day family members can check in and keep in touch, emotionally as well as physically. For a growing number of families with busy, diverse schedules, this one time to be together every day is fast disappearing.

Hectic family schedules and the decline of family mealtime have, no doubt, influenced the disappearance of family devotions. For past generations, the evening meal provided a daily gathering of the family and a natural time for the family to pause (usually after the meal) for brief prayer and Scripture reading. At our house we usually manage to eat together four nights a week, but we've largely given up any form of mealtime family devotions.

So what's the alternative? Is there some way we can carry on some spiritual nurture at home *in spite of* the pressures from the clock? We're going to answer that question in some detail in the chapter on family devotions, but for now it's enough to affirm once more that we can beat the clock. It just takes a little creativity.

There are many ways to take advantage of the everyday experiences of family life to powerfully shape our children's faith. We'll look closely at some of these in later chapters.

Learning to Beat the Clock

Job pressures, financial demands, and over-scheduling present real challenges to spending time with our families. That's the bad news. The good news is that some working parents *are* beginning to experiment with new ways to strike a healthy balance between work and family. They are discovering ways to carry on careers and *also* have time to enjoy each other and their children.[17]

The rapid increase of personal computers and fax machines at home has made telecommuting a real possibility for some parents. They are able to work some of the time at home so that they are more available to care for their children.

Others, having discovered new priorities, are stepping out of the "rat race." The former chief executive officer of a large commercial bank in Florida jumped off the fast track into a more "family-friendly" job. "I'm not naive enough to say that money doesn't matter. But I want my children to know me as something besides their provider," he said.[18] One working mother echoed the words of Scripture when she explained her cutback this way: "My career is important, but what have I gained if I lose my family?"[19]

For these and all families who really want to enjoy the fullness of what God offers them through family relationships, learning to beat the clock is both a priority and a necessity. Sharing time together (literally, sharing their lives) is a precious gift of love and trust that each family member gives to the others.

Second to a strong shared commitment to Christ, time together is the most crucial element in making families "work." A strong sense of family unity, belonging, and warmth doesn't just happen. It is nurtured and grown over time, just as a lovely garden flourishes in the hands of a caring, diligent gardener.

But let's be realistic for a moment. Life in this frantic society of ours is not likely to return to a much slower pace anytime soon. We can't turn back the clock. But neither do we have to settle for less than the best from our family life.

Families are discovering (and sometimes rediscovering) how to make time for each other every day. When they need more time together, they find ways to make it. And they're creatively inventing ways to make the most of the time they already have to build up and enjoy their families. We're going to share their secrets in the pages ahead.

These are families just like yours and mine. They live in the same world and face the same pressures from the clock that you and I do. But they've discovered ways to beat the clock and enjoy the rewards of family life.

Now that we've seen the challenges, it's time to draw up a battle plan for "beating the clock" so that you can begin to reap the rewards in your family, too!

_____

_____

_____

CHAPTER TWO

Beating the Clock: Making the Most of What You've (Already) Got

Most of us are already working hard at being with our families, and we aren't sure we could squeeze any more time for them out of our crazy schedules anyway. The secret is not necessarily to find *more* time for our families, but to make the most of the time we already have. That's what we're going to talk about now. Later, we'll explore some ways to find more time. We'll also look at how to use those extra-special occasions in family life to produce the greatest benefit for our families. But right now, our goal is simply to discover the time for our families that's *already there* in our daily schedules and to make the most of it!

Let's first look at the three most obvious times: bedtime, homework time, and mealtime. Perhaps you can think of other times particular to your family's life together. Even daily household chores and family projects such as remodeling, gardening, or serving meals at the city mission offer families rewarding times together doing activities you'd often give your time to anyway. That's the key to beating the clock: start with what you're already doing. Let's look at bedtime first.

Making the Most of Bedtime

When Dickens described life in revolutionary France as "the best of times . . . the worst of times," he could have been describing bedtime in any home with one or more young children. Bedtime can be a very warm and special end to the day for both parents and children. On the other hand, getting two or three (or more!) young children bathed, in their pajamas, through their stories and prayers, and into bed can require all the discipline and energy of running a marathon. And it can seem about as long!

But a young child's bedtime can also be a daily experience of life as the "best of times." It is a special time when they can sit on Mom's or Dad's lap and snuggle close as they listen to a story or just talk for a few minutes. Then, as they say their prayers to their loving heavenly Father, they are reminded of who they are and whose they are. Bedtime is a daily ritual that can affirm to our children our great love for them and how special they are to us and to God, whose love and care we represent.

But bedtime isn't special just for children. It's also a special opportunity for parents. At bedtime, children who have been seemingly impervious to parental advice and direction all day, can suddenly become receptive and compliant. At bedtime, even "big boys" who won't let their parents hug them all day, (such as my sixth-grader) want a "good night" hug and kiss. Bedtime can be a magical moment for both parents and children.

The problem is that this magical moment takes time. Two-career families, single parents, blended families, even "traditional" families—all struggle to find those few precious moments to spend with each child at the end of the day. How can they do it?

Two-parent families can rotate bedtime responsibilities so that over the course of a week each parent has put to bed each of the children at least a couple of times. Rotation can be planned and adjusted to compensate when one parent has to be out for several nights at bedtime.

For some families (especially single parents), separate bedtimes even fifteen minutes apart may be the answer (though I readily concede that may stretch out the bed-time "marathon" even more). Those few minutes when the parent can focus on each child individually provide a daily answer to a young child's often felt but seldom-voiced question: "Am I just one of the kids around here, or am I really someone special in this family?"

As fathers have begun to experience the many re-wards of parenting, they've come to realize that bedtime shouldn't be just for mothers anymore. A dad's presence is even more essential at bedtime if he is the parent who is away from home the most. His presence at bedtime helps to assure the child of the dependable care of both parents and of the reality and stability of the family unit. Single parents who make it a priority to be there for most bedtimes send their children the same important message.

Missing bedtime now and then is no cause for guilt. But what if you simply can't be there at bedtime with any regularity?

Perhaps your situation is like Tanya's. She's a single mom who works nights as a telephone operator. Even though she sees her son after school and before she goes to work, she uses her break to call him around bedtime.

It's a "check-in" and "good night" call all in one. In about ten minutes she can ask if he finished his homework and listen as he brings her up to date on his life since the school day ended. Her son knows she is "there" at bedtime and has affirmed her care for him, even though she must be at work.[1] In this instance, the telephone can be a parent's real friend.

A Special Ritual?

Bedtime can easily become just another daily chore. But it can be much more than that. Bedtime can become, both for child and parent, a daily ritual filled with all the symbolism and emotional and spiritual power of other family rituals such as weddings, family worship, and birthday parties.

It is precisely the regularity and predictability of bedtime, together with the parental expressions of love and affirmation, that make it an important time for children. The predictability and warmth of bedtime deepens a young child's faith that she is indeed very special to her parents and that her parents can be counted on to be there for her through the long night and once again in the morning. This is the beginning of a child's understanding of the totally dependable, unceasing love and care of God.

God's people have always known what an important ritual bedtime is. In Deuteronomy 6, where Moses instructs the Israelites in the spiritual nurture of their children, he specifically mentions bedtime ("when you lie down"). Israelite parents were told to use that time to remind their children of the things of the Lord: of His blessings during the day and His work in the past (through a Bible story). All of this was expressed with a prayer of thanks.[2]

Bedtime may only require a few minutes, especially as children get older. But potentially, it is time of the highest quality. Being there for those few minutes can help make up for absences during the rest of the day. Be there as often as you can, and make the most of it!

More Than a "Necessary Evil"

Mention the word *homework* to just about any child above second grade and his reaction is likely to be either a pained look or a loud groan. Usually homework is no fun. But it can be a really good and meaningful time between parent and child.

On the other hand, homework time can be just another of those "necessary evils" of family life, like bathing the dog or cleaning out the garage. Shouts of "Get that homework done this minute" and "But it's not fair!" don't exactly make for warm family feelings!

Since you're probably going to spend some time helping your children with their homework anyway, why not try to spend it in a positive, family-strengthening way?

As with so much in life, the key to success in this endeavor is perspective. It's helpful to see homework not as a tug-of-war between you and your child (one pulling to delay, one pulling to get it done), but as an opportunity for you and your child to work together as a team toward a common goal: completion of homework and progress toward good grades. As long as the participants can be patient with each other and the atmosphere is reasonably pleasant, common projects bind people together and reinforce their sense of family ties—even projects such as homework.

Using homework time as a family-strengthening activity does require some courage. It is much more successful if you begin by communicating clearly to your child your expectations about homework. This involves such parameters as when to get it done and the possibility that you may review its quality at any time on any night. You could say something like: "We both want you to do well. You'll be proud of yourself for your accomplishments. If you have problems, we can probably work them out together. I'll be glad to help in any way I can."

I make it a priority to be at home and available to help my sons with their homework at least three nights a week and, if necessary, at pre-arranged times on weekends. I'm also available to help them review for tests. I try to help with special papers and projects that are especially taxing. I don't do the work, but I can offer encouragement at key points in a long project, teach study skills, and show my overall interest.

All the experts agree that the children who are most successful in school are the ones whose parents show significant interest in their studies. Helping with homework—giving up time we could be reading or watching those televised sports events—underscores our interest and our commitment to the success of our children. It's time well spent!

Homework time is a regular opportunity for parents to offer their children encouragement and assistance. What child (or person of any age) doesn't need plenty of both? When a parent offers help in a positive way ("Let's see if we can figure this out together"), he gives a very practical demonstration of his love.

Now it's time for a confession. I know from experience how easy it is to lose patience during homework time. It's easy to stop encouraging and start sounding like a drill sergeant. It's easy to send out the message (unintentionally) that the reason for all this "help" is because your child's value is based on her academic success, not just because of who she is.

So be patient, keep cool, and keep your goal clearly in mind. When your attitude is "We're in this together, and we're going to win," homework time can mean a lot to your child.

Family Mealtime: Endangered Species?

Thanksgiving is always an experience to be anticipated in our family. For quite a few years now, my family and I have joined my parents, my brother, numerous aunts and uncles and their children and spouses (and assorted friends) for Thanksgiving dinner. There are usually twenty-five to thirty of us gathered at my uncle's house on the edge of my parents' dairy farm in northern New York state.

Three large wooden tables stretch out in one long, narrow room. The menu never varies. It's always ham (usually from pigs my uncle raises), turkey (sometimes homegrown), and freshly killed venison. The meal is always accompanied by lots of loud conversation, which tends to make it hard to hear the football game playing on the television facing the table. Now you can see why I call it an "experience."

Thanksgiving has become a real "gathering of the clan" for the Pattersons. As such gatherings often do, it reminds my sons and me of our roots, of those with whom we share a common heritage, and how much we all have to be thankful for. It is just about the only time of the year we'll all see each other and be able to get caught up on the life of the wider Patterson family.

In a smaller but no less real sense, that's what a daily family mealtime offers. A daily meal together, usually in the evening, is, as one observer described it, "the gathering place of the clan, the one time each day when parents and children are assured of uninterrupted time with each other."[3]

At least that's how it *should* work. The increasing complexity of family work schedules combined with the supermarket of after-school and evening activities for children make scheduling dinner together a feat worthy of a high-speed computer.

Today, about one-third of families no longer eat dinner together. And of the two-thirds that do, many give up any opportunity to have a meaningful conversation so that they can watch the evening news on television. But mealtime can be one of those special times to beat the clock.

Psychologist Lee Salk feels that a family mealtime is an "incredibly important daily appointment" and he decries its loss, especially for children.

> People used to talk and listen at family mealtime; but now they sit in front of the television set with their dinner. I don't care how busy you are; you can take that time with your children. You can talk about your dreams, you can talk about your day. You can talk about your frustrations. The busier you are, the more valuable mealtime is with your children. If we don't guard this time with our youngsters, they aren't going to develop healthy attitudes toward family life.[4]

Family mealtime may be the only "built-in" time for togetherness some families have in their daily schedule. For those twenty or thirty minutes, a family can "check-in" and renew their sense of togetherness. Obviously, family mealtimes offer more than just food for the body. They feed our spirits, also. At family mealtime, we are reminded of who we are: people who live together, love each other, and serve each other as we all serve Jesus Christ.

Mealtimes are rich in Christian imagery. From earliest history, eating together has been a central Christian ritual. The earliest celebrations of the Lord's Supper began with an actual meal,[5] and some Christian traditions still observe that "love feast" before taking the bread and the cup today. In the Gospels, Christ is a guest at many dinners. Even the biblical imagery of heaven is that of a banquet.[6]

A Family Sacrament

Korean Christians have a wonderful story they tell to their children that explains the difference between heaven and hell. It also emphasizes how rich an experience the simple act of eating together can be.

The story tells how the people in hell sit at a large table heavy with all kinds of fine food. Their punishment is that they are eternally unable to eat and enjoy the food because their chopsticks are seven feet long.

In heaven, the table and chopsticks are identical, but the people enjoy the feast. Why? They have discovered the joy of feeding each other![7] Family mealtimes remind us that the greatest joys in life are the ones that come from serving those we love.

A regular family mealtime is, in a real sense, a family sacrament. It feeds our bodies, emotions, and spirits, and it is a way we can celebrate our love for each other every day—or at least most days.

Sometimes insurmountable obstacles will cancel family mealtime. Don't feel guilty. Occasional clashes are unavoidable. But regular or deliberately scheduled infringements on the family dinner hour (work appointments or soccer practice, for example) are unacceptable. If your family schedule allows, you can deal with some of the pressures on family mealtime by keeping a "flexible" or "floating" dinner hour. Simply note everyone's schedule of evening activities for the week ahead and post the daily dinner hours for the whole week (which may change daily as evening schedules require).[8]

The keys to maintaining a family dinner time are flexibility in scheduling and firmness in fighting interruptions. Politely tell phone callers that you (or whomever the call is for) will call back after the meal. Don't let either the late breaking news or reruns of "The Cosby Show" interrupt your family sacrament.

Family mealtime is a special, daily opportunity for families to nourish each other. It's a sacred time, and it's one very important way to beat the clock.

Weekends Were Made for Families

If you are a single parent or have an especially time-consuming job, spending time with your children is always a special challenge. Weekends, when the children aren't in school and you aren't at work all day, is a prime time to be with your family.

The problem with Saturdays is that I always seem to have a long "Honey, Do" list. These are urgent projects that have been waiting all week for my attention. Perhaps that happens to you, too. However, all is not lost.

Often, it's possible to include at least one of your children in your errands and projects. We shouldn't mind the loss of some efficiency when the payoff is making the most of our weekend time to be with our children.

For a number of years, we lived in an area where there was an ice cream store two doors down from the hardware store. I could hardly visit the hardware store on Saturday without taking the boys along and stopping next door for a you-know-what. Visiting the hardware store always involved more than nuts and bolts!

When my boys were younger, I went through a three-year period where I worked three nights a week. So we developed a favorite Saturday morning ritual during those years. While Mom slept in, the boys and I would go out to an early breakfast at a local fast-food restaurant. The three of us looked forward to this time. We got back to the house around 9:00 A.M., and there was still plenty of morning left for projects.

One family I know schedules one Saturday morning a month for family outings and fun activities. You may prefer the afternoon if you like to sleep late. You can decide on the activity at the last minute, but the date should be scheduled on the family calendar well in advance. This will guard against inadvertantly scheduling a competing activity.

A variation on this practice is to schedule a "date" with each child once a month. Write it on the calendar so that if other invitations come, a parent can truthfully say, "I already have an appointment at that time."

An appointment with your children need not consume the whole day. A trip to the pizza shop, a movie, or a visit to the local museum are fine ways to keep a "date" with your child. The important thing is not what you do or even how long you spend doing it. The most important thing is that you do it together and enjoy each other in the process.

Not an Impossible Dream

These are just a few ways to maximize the time already in our schedules so that we can be with our families. You've probably already thought of others. Maybe you're even thinking about how to find some more time together. That's good. That's what healthy, happy families do. That's what makes them the way they are. They get together and enjoy each other as much and as often as possible.[9]

No one said beating the clock would be easy, but it can be done. It takes discipline to shut out the demands of our adult world and focus our energies and attention on our children. But that's what makes it "quality time," and with our quantity of time so short, we need all the quality we can get.

CHAPTER THREE

_____

_____

_____

Beating the Clock: Quality Time, Available Time

I was sitting in the office of the chief executive officer of a large, private foundation. I had requested an appointment to ask him for a grant. Before our conversation could get past the niceties, however, he took a phone call. Soon it became obvious he was talking to his son.

The call went on for nearly ten minutes, and I began to get a little resentful of the delay. After all, I was busy, too. This appointment was important to me, and I had prepared long and hard for it. Couldn't he talk to his son at home after work?

When the call was over, he explained to me, "My son is away at college. It's his first year. I told him that anytime he needs to talk to me, for any reason, just call. I'll be available. My secretary knows to always put him through to me. I can't be with him as much as I'd like now that he's away from home, but I can always be available to him when he needs me."

That father understood something very important: our availability to our children clearly reflects our priorities. This man's availability to talk with his son at any time during the work day communicated to his son that he was right at the top of his dad's list of priorities. The message he gave his son was "No one and no thing is more important to me than you are." That executive knew how to stay connected to his family even when he couldn't be with them.

We can't always be with our children when they or we would like. But here again, we don't have to feel beaten by the clock.

Refuse to Choose

In any discussion about spending time with our children, there's usually a debate over the relative merits of "quality" time and "quantity" time.

Family psychologist George Rekers illustrates the folly of trying to choose between quality and quantity time with our family. Imagine, he says, going into a fine restaurant and ordering the best steak they have. It's expensive. The waiter is impeccably dressed and serves your steak on fine china. But then you notice that your steak is only a one-inch cube. When you mention it to the waiter, he reminds you that it is the best steak available, and it is, after all, the quality, not the quantity that counts. That's all right unless you're hungry. Then you understand that quantity counts, too![1]

On the dairy farm where I grew up, we understood that it took a certain quantity of land to grow a certain amount of quality feed for the cows. Both quantity and quality were inextricably linked in the growth process.

It's the same with our families. When it comes to being with them, quality and quantity belong together. Even though I realize how true that is, I still find myself caught in a struggle with the clock to spend time with my sons. Some evenings I try to put down my work for ten to fifteen minutes to play a quick game with them. I usually enjoy the break, and they usually enjoy beating me!

Either Play the Game or Quit

I was in the middle of one of those quality-time games with my youngest son when suddenly he stopped playing to launch out on a seemingly endless, intricately detailed account of something that happened that day in school. "Come on, now," I said. "Either play the game or quit." All I wanted to do was get the game over so I could get back to my ever-so-much-more important work.

I was caught in the classic trap of a parent trying to spend a few stolen minutes of quality time with his child. My body was there, but my mind was somewhere else. In reality I was not emotionally available to my son. I was not really "there" to be with him and enjoy him.

When our children ask for our time, they offer us a precious gift. They tell us how much they love us, how special we are to them, and how much they need us.

What wonderful affirmation! And by accepting their gift, we return that same affirming love.

When we accept their request to shut out our world and join them in theirs for those few minutes, we tell them how valued and special they are to us. In those few minutes together, we affirm our mutual love in a concrete, practical way through the gift of our time and our undivided attention.

No such time with our children is ever wasted, no matter what the game, no matter how childlike the play.[2] Yet, giving time is no easy thing with the incessant demands of the clock ticking in our ears. And what about those times when we really can't be with them?

When All Else Fails, Telephone

It happens to even the most committed, best organized parent sooner or later. The late afternoon meeting runs past quitting time. The boss wants that important report "yesterday." Rush hour traffic is backed up to Alaska.

Your carefully arranged schedule is useless. There's just no way you can get home, eat dinner with the family, and make it to that special school concert or sports event.

That's when it's time to take a deep breath and remember that after the first three or four years of life, our children can survive and even flourish without us being with them every minute of the day. They may well benefit from a regular, out-of-home play school experience to help them develop socially. They can visit playmates in other homes for short visits, too.

Early in life, our children develop to where they don't need us every minute, but they do need us when they "need" us. Often when they are navigating the passages of daily life, they need us for advice, reassurance, or just some of that focused attention that assures them of our love.

If we can't always be there physically—and let's face it, we can't—they still need to know that we are available to them emotionally. Here's where the telephone becomes a parent's friend. The same instrument that seems to be permanently attached to a teenager's ear can also help us be available to our children when they need us.

A scene from the popular movie *Baby Boom*, starring Diane Keaton, illustrates this. Keaton plays J.C. Wiatt, a successful management consultant. In one especially funny scene, Wiatt is making a sales presentation to an all-male group in the conference room when the phone rings. It's Wiatt's baby-sitter calling. She can't find the nipples for the baby bottle.

Wiatt is obviously embarrassed and the men in the room chuckle and grin as they listen to her increasingly exasperated conversation. Things just get worse when the baby comes on the line and wants her mother to sing a chorus of "Itsy Bitsy Spider."

Certainly the movie overplays the situation for laughs, but it does make a point. As a result of the demands of the clock, both parents and children rely more and more on the one fixture in their homes that allows them to "reach out and touch" each other emotionally when they can't be together physically: the telephone.

The After-School Connection

The telephone is especially useful during that after-school period when many working parents fight the "Three O'Clock Syndrome." That's the daily anxiety attack that afflicts working parents about ten minutes after their children are supposed to arrive home from school.[3]

"I just need to know they are home," said one working mother of her eleven- and twelve-year-old children. "By 3:10 P.M. I start calling and getting real nervous." A call from her children with a simple "Hi, Mom. I'm home" is all she needs to relieve her anxiety.[4]

Children often call a parent at work to relieve their own anxieties too. Sometimes they just need the reassurance of hearing their parent's voice. Jay Belsky, a recognized child development expert and professor at Pennsylvania State University, feels that "the issue is not so much if someone is there when a child gets home from school as whether someone is there psychologically for the child. Does he have someone to call if he needs something? . . . The psychological connection is more important than the physical one."[5]

Kids also call their parents at work for help with things parents would do if they were right in the same room. This includes such exciting tasks as solving sibling quarrels ("Jenny won't let me . . .") and cheering them up after one of life's major tragedies ("Johnny broke up with me today").

Since all of us don't have the freedom that my friend, the foundation executive, has to set our own telephone priorities at work, these calls often require us to summon up all the parental wisdom we can muster.

Ellen Galinsky, project director of the Work and Family Life Studies Program at the Bank Street College in New York City, says that if you didn't witness what happened at home, it is sometimes better to delay any judgment of guilt or innocence and refuse to settle sibling quarrels.

Instead, insist they work out their problems between them (unless you can see a clear danger or problem that requires immediate attention).[6]

As with any good thing, keeping in touch with our children by phone can be overdone, especially by them. The author of an article called "Hello, Could I Talk to My Mom, Please?" says that if your children are calling you at work frequently, it may be that you are relying too much on the phone in your relationship with them. They may be trying to tell you they need more of your personal, eye-to-eye attention in the evenings and on weekends.[7]

About twice a month, a conference or speaking engagement takes me away from home for a few nights. Then, the telephone is my valued partner in making me available to my wife and children. We've never had a set rule about it, but I usually call every evening around dinner time, as my schedule permits. As a parent of two hungry, healthy sons, I know with certainty where my sons will be at that time.

That call lets me give undivided attention to both boys and my wife. I ask the boys about their day and put in the necessary reminder about homework. I usually get a chance to share about my day too.

Sometimes, a phone call while we're at work or on the road provides our children with a sympathetic, parental ear and the assurance (especially for the youngest children) that we haven't disappeared. If we use the telephone to listen carefully, to be properly sympathetic and genuinely interested in our children (spouses, too), the telephone can be a very valuable tool.

Let me repeat one caution: A phone call is no substitute for spending time with the people we love. When

that's not possible, however, it can be the next best thing.
It can help our families maintain a sense of togetherness
and availability to each other in spite of busy schedules.
Sometimes, believe it or not, the telephone is a parent's
best friend.

_____

_____

_____

CHAPTER FOUR

Beating the Clock: Growing a Happy Marriage

I remember how strange it looked to me as a teenager. I'd go with my parents to a church dinner and, invariably, all the married couples would be sitting together for the meal. *They could sit together all the time at home,* I thought. *Why didn't they take the opportunity to sit with other people? Wouldn't that be more exciting?*

Twenty-two years of marriage has changed my perspective. What seemed so strange then is normal behavior now. Whoever said "When two or three are gathered together, somebody spills the milk," must have been thinking of mealtime with small children! Now I understand just how special it is to be able to sit together and talk during a meal without having to cut up anyone's food or clean up spilled milk. I understand how the sense of closeness and belonging together doesn't fade, but may grow even stronger when a couple goes "out."

My perspective isn't the only thing that's changed over the years. More than ever, it seems that time just to be with our spouses, is increasingly rare. Opportunities to enjoy each other's company, to just sit together and talk, or to get a late-night snack together after the kids are in bed come all too infrequently.

Yet, everyone who is married, or ever hopes to be married, wants a happy marriage. One shrewd observer noted that "Nothing in life gives people as much happiness as a good marriage and as much misery as a bad one."[1] That's one reason behind the high divorce rate today. People won't settle for just being married. They want to be happy, and they're determined to keep trying until they get it right.

That's really no surprise, is it? A happy marriage is a well-spring of sustenance, healing, and growth. From such a marriage, we receive daily the sustenance and support of someone who truly cares for us. Our spouse's affection and acceptance helps heal the wounds we bear from childhood. These gifts enable us to believe that we are loved and valued, that we are someone who matters and truly "belongs."

Personal *growth* comes from the security of a "predictable partner," a loving companion who is always there to encourage us to develop our gifts and talents, with all the satisfaction that brings us.[2] These are precious gifts we can give our spouses daily.

This daily gift-giving, "in bed and over the breakfast table,"[3] is the stuff of which lasting, satisfying love is made. Marriage counselors describe this kind of love as an "intimate partnership"[4] and a "companionship love."[5]

In practical terms, it's the kind of love shared by a Nebraska couple married for thirty-seven years. "We're more than married," they said, "we're best friends." This couple, and so many others like them have become "mates, lovers, companions, partners, and best friends." They happily affirm that the "central satisfaction" of their lives is their relationship.[6]

Will the Garbage Win?

Happily married couples invariably report that they "grow" their marriages in a number of specific ways. One way is by spending time together. And they do it "over the long haul." That Nebraska couple has been at it for thirty-seven years!

A happy marriage begins with a lifetime commitment. From a biblical perspective, commitment is the basis for love between a man and a woman, not the other way around. Ideally, love and marriage *should* go together, but biblically, the marriage commitment takes priority over love. Tim Stafford puts it this way: "The cup is necessary before the wine is poured."[7]

An "instant" intimate marriage partnership is as impossible as becoming an "instant adult." Perhaps microwaves can produce instant dinners, but nothing can produce instant intimacy. It is the "patient and deliberate dedication to the happiness and well-being of another person," (Christians call it love) applied daily over the years, that enables a marriage to yield its rich rewards.[8]

Nick Stinnett and John De Frain, in their book *Secrets of Strong Families*,[9] tell the story of an Arkansas couple who attended a weekend marriage enrichment seminar. The leader asked the couple two questions: "How many minutes do you spend each day taking out the garbage?" and "How many minutes do you spend each day in conversation?" You've already guessed the result, I'm sure. The garbage took about five minutes each day and the garbage won![10]

How can we be sure the garbage doesn't "win" in the daily struggle for our time? Is there any way we can use the precious minutes we have to build a strong, happy marriage? There is no easy answer, but there is a way. It lies in the daily practice of some important marriage disciplines.

The Daily Disciplines of Marriage

Suppose we went on a cross-country trip and stopped frequently along the way to talk with couples who have strong, happy marriages. We'd sit with them and ask about their habits and all aspects of their daily lives. What do you suppose we'd learn?

My guess is that we'd find these lasting, rewarding marriages share at least one common characteristic: discipline. We'd discover that these couples have intentionally built into their lives little habits, daily disciplines, that (in spite of the pressures of the clock) enable their marriages to grow and deepen over the years.

Many of these couples would be surprised to hear us speak of their actions as "disciplines." Their lives are as busy as yours and mine. They don't have big blocks of time to just sit and gaze into each other's eyes.

However, they have discovered the value of some small things, done regularly, that make a big diference in their marriages. These daily habits and practices have become a normal part of everyday married life for them.

What are these disciplines? They are keeping in touch, daily grace, growing together, and growing in faith. Let's look at each one individually.

The Discipline of Keeping in Touch

My wife and I have said it to each other many times. "It seems like I hardly knew you when we first got married." And after twenty-two years together, we realize how true that was.

The day we spoke our marriage vows, two strangers stepped into a strange new world together. We started on a journey that we hoped would last a lifetime and bring us great joy and satisfaction. We couldn't know then that we would find ourselves literally re-created and redefined in the daily giving and receiving of our married life.[11]

For most of us, marriage starts not only with high hopes but also with more than just a dash of romance. Those early days together are sweetened by the romantic glow and excitement of beginning something tremendous together. There's "just the two of us," and it's great!

Sooner or later, however, reality sets in. It's usually linked to the arrival of children. Parenthood changes everything. Suddenly, we are responsible for this helpless little person. We are no longer primarily on the receiving end of nurture from our spouse but become nurturers ourselves. That can be quite a shock!

The demands of family life increase from year to year, and often so do our career responsibilities. One day, we may realize that we don't spend time on the "little things" of daily family life, such as conversation or just being available to listen in a caring way.

"We never talk anymore."

"Okay, what do you want to talk about?"

"I don't know; I just want to talk."

Does that sound familiar? We've had that conversation in our home. Perhaps you've had it in yours too.

Even if you do set aside time to talk, it may seem as if there's nothing to talk about![12] That "stranger" you married so many years ago and determined to have as your best friend is still (or once again) a stranger. If we let that happen, we've lost touch with each other. The clock has won!

Can we avoid the trap of losing touch with each other? Of course we can. Couples who avoid this trap practice the daily discipline of keeping in touch through conversation (talking *and* listening) with each other.

Conversation includes, of course, the perfunctory "How was your day?" that covers the "battle report" on daily life. But it goes far beyond that. Our spirits become "knit together" as we share, however briefly, our "ideals, fears, hopes, doubts, and longings"[13] and our experiences of God's daily care. And don't neglect the progress reports on braces, soccer games, and that big sales presentation. They're important, too.

It takes effort to do this regularly; effort just to keep involved enough and interested enough in each other "[to] anticipate what to ask, what to talk about, and when." It takes a real desire to keep each other filled in on the changes in our lives. That's why we call it a discipline.

But this shared conversation, involving "little things" as well as hopes and dreams, serves us well. It deepens and enriches each couple's unique and shared "emotional repertoire."[14] Spouses can't be best friends, partners, and companions without it.

Does this talk of a daily discipline sound too challenging? It needn't. As little as five minutes of conversation after work is a good beginning. A cup of tea together after dinner (before the dishes, the evening paper, or the television) or getting into bed a few minutes early to allow for some "pillow talk" are simple ways you can practice the discipline of keeping in touch with your spouse.

"God gave you two ears and one mouth so you could listen twice as much as you talk." That advice from parents to children is good advice for marriage partners too. Keeping in touch goes well beyond just talking together or even knowing what to say. The discipline of keeping in touch in marriage requires "listening to the heart" of our spouse so that we can discover together a "common heart".[15] This is the loving listening of two people on a journey toward a deep friendship and love. Each must listen to the other in order to find the way.[16]

Keeping in touch has a more literal aspect. Jesus often put his hands on people as a means of blessing them and showing his love and care. Touch can be a powerful communicator of those emotions. A daily hug (or two!) is tonic to a mate's spirit. A loving hug (or pat on the bottom!) helps keep romance alive and growing. Practice "keeping in touch" with your spouse this way every day.

Just as we practice discipline in our work and in our spiritual lives, we must practice the discipline of keeping in touch in married life. This kind of discipline is essential to growing a true "companionship love" in your marriage. Talk together, listen to each other, and keep in touch.

The Discipline of Daily Grace

In his book, *On This Day*, Carl D. Windsor tells the story of a grandmother who was celebrating her golden wedding anniversary. Inevitably, someone asked her the secret of her long and happy marriage. She explained, "On my wedding day, I decided to make a list of ten of my husbands faults, which for the sake of our marriage, I would overlook."

When she was asked what some of those faults were, she replied, "To tell you the truth, my dear, I never did get around to listing them. But whenever my husband did something that got me hopping mad, I would say to myself, 'Lucky for him that's one of the ten!' "[17]

Now that was a lady who was wise in the things of marriage! She knew the need for a large amount of grace daily to keep her marriage long and happy.

Grace is central to the success of any marriage, especially one between Christians. Spouses who practice this discipline daily nurture their marriages with the soft, gentle rain of God's grace that refreshes our spirits and nourishes our mutual love as well as our love for Him.

"Great occasions for serving God come seldom, but little ones surround us daily." I keep that saying on my desk in my study as a reminder of the necessity of showing God's grace to my spouse every day. Rarely, if ever, will I be able to play the "hero" for my wife, but there are many small, yet significant opportunities to serve God and show her His grace (and my love) every day.

It only takes a particularly stressful time, a hard day or week at work, or caring for a houseful of young children for two consecutive rainy days to remind us how much the loving ministry of one spouse to another, the "pitching in," and the thoughful gesture mean to our marriage. They truly are "nothing less than a means of grace" from one spouse to the other.[18]

My wife is a public school teacher, and my office is at home. Most mornings, she has to rush out of the house and into her car for the drive to work, while I "commute" down the hall to my study. So, if she is savoring a longer "quiet time" or just hurrying to get dressed, I try to have a hot bowl of cereal waiting when she's ready for it. That saves her five minutes and doesn't increase my commute at all.

My wife has many ways of ministering grace to me, too. For example, she knows I don't enjoy doing yard and home repair work, so she often does them without even asking me to help. Now that's true grace!

Having his morning coffee and paper ready when he comes to the table or her car filled with gas the night before so that she doesn't have to leave for work earlier the next morning are wonderful and undeserved reminders of our spouse's love.

This ministry of grace to our spouse is as much a disci-pline as that of keeping in touch. It's natural to focus on our own needs and the incessant demands of life. The discipline of daily grace, by contrast, requires "the patient and deliberate dedication to the happiness and well-being" of our spouse every day. That is the essence of Christian love and is essential to a happy Christian marriage.[19]

The discipline of daily grace involves more than just service to our spouse. It also involves accepting and forgiving our spouse on a daily basis.

My wife keeps a very livable but neat house. The atmosphere is relaxed, the furniture is functional. The house can be lived in and enjoyed (even by our children), and, somehow, it remains neat.

To me, however, a house should have a newspaper or two scattered around the living room chair and a few magazines casually spread around on any place big enough to hold them. I call that "livable." My wife calls it "messy." I have even been told that my desk looks like someone dumped his garbage on it. But it feels comfortably "livable" to me.

You can see the potential for sharp disagreement here. As a result, every day of our marriage, my wife has had many opportunities to show me grace by accepting my penchant for a "relaxed" home atmosphere. And I have had the opportunity to show her grace by trying to be a bit neater. That's the way it is for most of us. Grace is a daily act of loving and accepting our spouses—messiness and all.

This grace we offer our spouses is a reflection of God's grace shown to us. After all, God does not wait until we are perfect to love us. That's what makes His grace so gracious. Loving our mates means having a similar gracious willingness to love and accept them for who they are, without demanding that they first be perfect.

Grace and Perspective

Farmers and diamond miners move a lot of dirt in the course of a day, but their perspective is quite different. The farmer's main focus is on the dirt itself as he prepares it for the crops. The diamond miner moves the dirt too, but his attention is focused on the occasional diamond he finds there. He sees his work from the perspective of one concerned for the diamonds, not the dirt.[20]

That's a helpful way to think about marriage and family life. What we look for in our spouse (or children) often determines what we find. There is inevitably a lot of "dirt" to be sorted through in marriage, a lot of bad habits, disagreements, and the like. It's all a matter of perspective.

Practicing the discipline of daily grace toward our spouse doesn't necessarily mean we ignore the dirt. It just helps us keep it in perspective. It helps us keep our attention focused on the diamonds in our marriage: a caring spouse, a growing relationship, and daily acts of love and sharing.

My messiness is just one of the pieces of dirt that my wife has to move around in our marriage. I have also been accused of having a looser attitude toward spending our money (usually money not yet earned) than is healthy for the family finances. On the other hand, it has taken me most of our married life to get used to my wife's habit of rearranging the furniture every six months. Having my chair, couch, and bed in the same place for years on end represents security and stability for me. For my wife, such sameness means staleness and sterility.

So each of us has had to accept the fact that the other is far from perfect. Failure and disappointment is an inevitable part of married life, and we've both had to learn to practice the daily graces of acceptance and forgiveness.

At the very center of God's "unmerited favor" to us is His willingness, even eagerness, to forgive us daily. We don't want to disappoint Him. We don't want to fail Him. But, in this life, perfection is impossible. We live by His grace.

So it is with our marriages. Perfection is too heavy a burden for any spouse to bear. A critical, unaccepting, unforgiving attitude by one spouse leads to the other feeling unappreciated and unloved—like a project someone has to "fix." Sooner or later, that spouse's spirit is crushed, and he or she could become vulnerable to finding the gifts of sustenance, healing, and growth outside the marriage. It's *not* excusable, but it *is* understandable.

Daily applications of acceptance and forgiveness heal a spouse's bruised spirit. Even better, they keep it healthy and promote its growth. Together with the grace of service, acceptance and forgiveness are special ways we can minister grace to our spouses daily.

These graces may not come easily to some of us. That's why we call them disciplines. But the opportunities to practice them surround us just as dirt surrounds diamonds. It's all a matter of perspective.

The Discipline of Growing Together

For weeks it was the subject of screaming tabloid headlines and features on the evening news. Billionaire Donald Trump and his wife, Ivana, were getting a divorce. Here was a couple who seemed to have everything. What was the problem?

"People just grow apart," Trump said.[21] Both Donald and Ivana were very busy people in very stressful careers. He spent his married life amassing his fortune; she spent hers managing one of his major hotels. Both of them were too busy or too stressed (or both) to spend time growing together. So they just grew apart.

Trump was right. People *do* grow apart (especially marriage partners) unless they intentionally work at growing together. Few of us are as wealthy as the Trumps, but our lives are not that different in this respect: time pressures from our careers and other commitments challenge us to find time to be with each other. Yet that's exactly how marriages are nurtured. That's how spouses grow together.

Time together is certainly a "gift we give each other," as well as a discipline.[22] Like any discipline, it can produce significant results. Here are some ways to begin.

Time Together: It's "Doable"

After a shared commitment to Christ, regular time together with your spouse is a basic ingredient in growing together in marriage. After all, how else are you going to become best friends with that "stranger" you married?

Although we're all pressured by the clock, making time for each other doesn't have to be a major operation. Sometimes all that's needed is a few minutes together over coffee (after the children have left the table) or doing the dinner dishes together (automatic dishwashers save time but may not be so good for marriages). That "endangered species," the family mealtime, isn't just good for the children. It provides a built-in daily time to check in with our spouse, too. It's already part of the day. Why not make use of it?

I'll admit that I'm like most husbands in two-paycheck families. Much of the time, I'm guilty of not doing my share of the housework. But I really don't mind cleaning. There is something wonderfully therapeutic for me about running the vacuum cleaner. It's also a chore that matches my household skills perfectly! So, during the weekly Saturday morning cleaning at our house, I may run the vacuum. That makes cleaning the house something we do together. It's no longer mundane or routine; it's time we share working together. And we enjoy it.

Let's Make a Date

When I was a child, going out for ice cream was one of our family's favorite activities. I can eat ice cream any time, any place. I still have a picture of myself as a student eating an ice cream cone in Red Square in Moscow on New Year's Eve when the temperature was well below zero.

Going for an ice cream cone was always such a treat. I remember, however, that it wasn't long before I began to wish for more than just one scoop on a cone. The ice cream was so good, I wanted a big, delicious sundae!

Daily times with our mates are like those delicious single-dip cones. They're always special, but they also whet our appetite for longer, "just the two of us" times together. These big delicious "sundaes" are what spouses call "dates."

Bob and Cheryl have been married for over twenty-five years. They've had plenty of opportunity to grow apart in their relationship, or at least get pretty stale. But they still hold hands a lot, they laugh together, and they clearly enjoy being with one another. What's their secret? Throughout their marriage, they've kept Friday evening open just for each other. It's their time to be together, and sometimes to go on a date.[23]

Bob and Cheryl are living illustrations of the importance of regularly and intentionally making time to be together. They value that regular, weekly date because they have learned from experience that "there's nothing like a good date with your mate to revive the most important relationship in your life. Whether going out together for an entire evening or staying in your own backyard, time alone as a couple—without the kids, phone calls, or newspapers to distract you—can do wonders for keeping kindled the flame of marital love."[24]

Did you notice the part about "without the kids"? That can be the hardest part of arranging a date. Every parent knows that finding the time, money, and energy to focus on each other can seem impossible when you have young children.

Here's some sound, straightforward advice: do whatever you have to.[25] Plan ahead. Write the date in your calendar so that work and other obligations can't easily interfere. Budget for a baby-sitter once a week or twice a month. Try to get away together a couple of times each year for a night or weekend.

Some couples enjoy spending time together on a joint project such as serving meals at the city mission, restoring old furniture, or just doing yard work together.

We live in New York State not far from the border of Massachusetts and Vermont. We take every opportunity we can to drive over and explore the beautiful New England towns close by.

A date with your spouse can be a lot of fun and is limited only by your own creativity. For instance, you can take a candle lit bath together some evening; sit outside in the moonlight together; get up fifteen minutes earlier tomorrow (before the children) and have a cup of coffee and pray together; take a bike ride, visit a local museum, or go grocery shopping together (there's a way to beat the clock!). Go window shopping at the mall or out to breakfast on Saturday. Go for a walk in the snow and take a hot shower together after you get home.[26]

Marriage counselors all agree on this: "It's a very good idea to have some time together every single day, and no time is better spent than a few minutes focusing on our spouse each day."[27] Just a *few* minutes having fun together and enjoying each other regularly helps us beat the clock's relentless pressure to grow apart.

Donald Trump was only partly right. People don't need to "just grow apart." Instead, they can grow *together* in an ever deepening love and companionship.

So why not begin the discipline of growing together in marriage now? Remember: small, regular investments grow and yield large rewards.

The Discipline of Growing in Faith

The divorce epidemic that has swept our country in recent decades has also ravaged the church. But it is still true that "the family that prays together, stays together." A strong faith contributes significantly to successful, happy marriages and family relationships.[28]

I believe it is a spiritual principle: *As you deepen your discipleship, you strengthen your marriage.* Nothing creates such a strong and lasting bond between two people as a deeply held and shared allegiance to Jesus Christ. On the other hand, not to share this faith with your spouse would be, as one lady described it, "like living with an alien."[29]

The source of all the daily graces we strive to practice in our marriages is tapped as we nurture our own trust in and obedience to the One who is the source of all grace—Jesus Christ. He is the One who came not to be served, but to serve.

A Romans 8:28 Family

Less than ten miles from our house lives a Christian family whose five-year-old son has cancer. He is undergoing chemotherapy. No one but God knows what the outcome will be.

Such a situation has torn apart many marriages. However, I'm confident this one will survive. It may even grow stronger as a result.

So what's the difference here? This couple knows they are not alone in their struggle. Christians across the entire area are praying for them. They know they are not powerless in their battle. As a result, they are able to maintain a confident attitude and strong faith. They are an example of what I call a "Romans 8:28 Family." They know that God does, indeed, work all things together for good for His people. What strength that adds to their marriage, and right at the point where they need it most!

How can you and I nurture a similar vital, shared faith? How can we beat the clock and all its pressures to wear down our marriages and pull them apart? Some couples start the day ten or fifteen minutes earlier so that they can sing a hymn or song of praise together as a couple (or family).[30] Other couples pray and have a daily quiet time with God, either together or individually.

Couples who are growing together in faith make it a priority to worship together, especially in public. They live out their faith through the rituals and traditions of the many seasons of the church year. In this way, they develop a shared faith history and identity as a couple.

These couples don't just "talk" their faith, they "walk" it too. They serve their Lord together at the community soup kitchen or homeless shelter, by leading a Bible study for couples in their neighborhood, by being sponsors of their church's youth group, or by having a ministry of service and encouragement to single parents.

In these and countless other ways, couples nurture their own faith as individuals and are bound together by the shared service of obedience they give their Lord. In many cases, they'd be doing these things anyway; they just do them together.

These couples also undertake the task of sharing their growing faith with their children. And they do it in the most effective way ever discovered: by being models for their children and teaching them through daily life together as a family. We'll talk about that in more detail in a later chapter. Right now, it's enough to recognize that this task alone is enough to keep any couple "on their toes" and growing together spiritually.

If you feel you've been too busy and have not put enough effort into growing together in faith with your spouse, don't despair. It's never too late. The important thing is to start. God will honor your faithful efforts. Just start now, in any way you can.

If you're starting "from scratch," perhaps you'll need to begin by having a daily time of reading the Bible and prayer. If your spouse doesn't share that daily discipline, be patient. Share with him or her how much it means to your daily growth in faith. Let me remind you again of the spiritual principle at work here: *As you deepen your discipleship, you strengthen your marriage.*

Many times, practicing a discipline begins with following a set of priorities. As a way of building a stronger marriage (and family life) and a deeper, shared faith with your spouse, I suggest that you adopt the following priorities:

#1: Your relationship with God

#2: Your relationship with your spouse

#3: Your relationship with your children

#4: Your relationship with your work

If you keep those priorities straight and determine to spend your time in a way that reflects them, you may not spend more time, but the time you do spend will make every minute count for the things in life that really matter. Isn't that what life (and beating the clock) is all about?

PART TWO

Winning over the Long Haul

CHAPTER FIVE

_____

_____

_____

"Family Devotions? You Must Be Kidding!"

Driving home from work, Dad remembers that tonight is the night each week his family lingers around the dinner table for brief family devotions. He's looked through a devotional booklet over the weekend, so he's prepared. In fact, he's looking forward to it. It feels good to have the family together once a week for this special worship time.

Then just before dinner, the phone rings. "Dad, I'm over at Jim's," his teenager says. "They invited me for dinner, and since I was coming over at 7:00 P.M. for that study group meeting anyway, I think it's a good idea to stay. There's a big test tomorrow. I told you last week, remember?"

Dad doesn't remember, but he doesn't protest much either. It seems like his teenager is always finding some excuse to miss family devotions, even though it's only once a week. *Well, we'll just have to go ahead without him,* he thinks.

But when dinner time arrives, Mom hasn't come home yet. She must be caught in freeway traffic again. So Dad and his young daughter eat together. At least the two of them can share devotions. A little one-on-one time will be good for them.

Just as Dad puts down his fork and reaches for the Bible, the doorbell rings. "Can Jenny come out and play?" a small voice asks. "Please, Dad, I never get to play with my friends. Besides, it'll be dark soon and I'll have to do my homework."

So Dad sighs, resigns himself to the inevitable, and prepares for "family" devotions alone. He knows he ought to have family devotions, but sometimes he gets pretty discouraged. Sometimes he wonders if it's worth the effort.

That fictional family illustrates some of the challenges that face parents who want to have family devotions. There are so many other activities—homework, playtime, chores, television, evening meetings—competing for those few, brief minutes. Combined with disinterest from some family members, they tend to "squeeze out" family devotions from an already hectic family schedule.

One study estimates that only 5 percent of Christian families actually have regular family devotions together.[1] Most of the other 95 percent are probably like your family and mine. They try and fail and try (and fail) again and only fitfully manage to have some family devotions before giving up in frustration and guilt.

What's the solution? Is the only alternative to resign ourselves to failure and give up? Some parents decide to entrust the spiritual education of their children to their church's Sunday school or even to a Christian school. In these settings, at least, there is regularly scheduled time for studying the Bible and worship. After all, the teachers are equipped and trained to do this kind of thing. Doesn't it make sense to let them do what they do best and relieve busy families of one more demand on their time?

When I was a boy growing up on a dairy farm, I was responsible for helping my dad with the daily chores. One of my chores was cleaning the milking equipment every evening. Dad explained to me that the equipment had to be cleaned thoroughly or bacteria would grow in the equipment overnight and contaminate the milk during milking the next day.

He carefully showed me how to clean the milking machines with the disinfectant solution. It seemed like such an endless task! And there were always neighborhood boys waiting to play. So one evening I just rinsed the equipment quickly, put it in its place, and ran off to play.

The next day an entire shipment of milk (and a lot of money) had to be poured "down the drain" because the bacteria count was too high. The milk processing company wouldn't accept it. Then Dad and I went to work washing everything even more thoroughly and more carefully than before. I didn't get to play that evening at all!

I learned an important lesson from that. It may take a long time to do things right, but it takes longer to do them over.

That lesson applies to family devotions too. If we're going to do it, we need to invest the time and energy. If we don't, we may miss altogether our God-given opportunity as parents to nurture our children's spiritual growth. And we only get one chance. This is one job we don't get the opportunity to do over.

No Substitutes Will Do

Sunday school and Christian schools have their place, but there's no substitute for the home in shaping and nurturing faith and spiritual growth in our children. In fact, this has been God's intention from the beginning.

This was the core of what Moses, the great leader of Israel, told his people as they prepared to live as free families after their deliverance from slavery in Egypt. Moses told parents that he would teach them all of the principles, laws, and decrees of God so that they and their children might revere and obey Him as long as they lived. Speaking on behalf of the Lord, Moses promised the people that as long as they and their children obeyed the Lord, they would be richly blessed.[2]

What was the first step in assuring this blessing for them and their children? First, Moses told them to take all of God's commands "to heart"; he told them to incorporate God's commands into their own lives and then to "impress them on their children." After that, Moses gave the people specific examples of how to do that, and every example he gave had to do with everyday home and family life.[3] That's where the most effective "Christian education" of children takes place.

A child's parents are the first and most effective means of helping a child develop his understanding of God, what someone has called a child's "God-concept." Your "God-concept" is a way of describing the "lens through which you see God and through which you believe He sees you." This understanding of God, which parents help their child to form, in turn forms his understanding of the purpose and meaning of his life and life in general.[4]

If our children see God as a living, loving father who cares about them and the world at large, it is because such a "God-concept" has most likely been developed in the home. If a negative image of God develops in a child, it can be "undone" later, but like my experience with the milking equipment, it's a lot easier to "do it right" the first time. Undoing a person's "God concept" can be a long and painful task.

Nowhere is this more evident than in the life of Martin Luther. Hans Luther, Martin's father, was a harsh, distant, and authoritarian man. His stern presence cast a dark pall over the entire family atmosphere. For young Luther, his father became the embodiment of a cold, distant, and angry God.

Luther carried this "God-concept" into his adult life. Just as he never felt loved or accepted by his father, he did not feel loved or accepted by God. Though he became a priest, he lived with the terrible fear that he was destined to be an object of God's wrath, never to be redeemed. This warped "God-concept" shaped Luther's self-image. His self-esteem suffered terribly. He lived with tremendous guilt and self-hate.

It was only after much emotional and spiritual agony and struggle that Luther finally was able to break the chains of his childhood concept of God. While he was reading Paul's epistle to the Romans one day, God's grace finally broke through to Luther. He realized that God did love him and freely offered him forgiveness by faith. After much pain and struggle, he was "able to forgive God for being a father, like his own." Finally, Luther felt free to be loved and accepted by God.[5]

In the daily experiences of family life, our children learn to know God and how to honor and obey him. This is also the pattern in the New Testament. Entire families were sometimes converted to faith and then instructed in the faith together. This teaching often took place in the home ("from house to house")[6] as well as in the Temple.

When a family grows in faith together, believing parents feel confident of raising believing children.[7] This was the case of Paul's protégé, Timothy, who had been taught the faith from his earliest days by his mother and grandmother.[8]

The first presidential campaign I can remember was in 1960 when John F. Kennedy beat Richard Nixon. I was only twelve years old, but I was a fervent Nixon supporter. Was my support based on my careful analysis of the relative positions of the two candidates? Hardly. Did it stem from a basic commitment to a party (as is the case with many, if not most voters)? Not at all. My vocal support for Nixon as a twelve-year-old was based on only one thing: the fact that my father, who was a long-time Republican office holder, supported Nixon. I simply adopted my dad's political values as my own. I didn't understand why my father supported Nixon, but I knew he did. Our whole family did. So that became my attitude also.

So it is with spiritual values. If we are people who practice the disciplines of regular, personal Bible study and prayer, make it a priority to be in church on Sunday, and demonstrate a spirit of generosity toward those in need and reconciliation toward those with whom we have differences, then our children will be much more likely to incorporate those same traits into their own identities as members of the family. Those attitudes, values, and disciplines will be part of what it means to be "Pattersons" or "Joneses" or whatever your family name is.

It is our responsibility to nurture our children's faith in the home. But there are still the intimidating obstacles of time pressures, conflicting schedules, and just plain indifference. Can we beat the clock in this crucial area too? Indeed, we can.

There are three approaches to spiritual nurture in the home that families use today with varying degrees of success. One is a modern version of the traditional "family altar." Another is a more recent innovation, the weekly "family night." The third is what I call the "family atmosphere" approach.

We'll discuss each one in detail and offer some help in applying them so that you can judge which approach or combination of approaches might work best for your family. Each approach takes time, but it also meets our main criterion of offering maximum returns to your family in exchange for the investment of your limited time. Let's look at each approach separately now.

Family Devotions

This family time of spiritual nurture has been called the "family altar" or family devotions. It's a long-standing (though often challenging) way to nurture the faith of your children. It's easiest to start when your children are young so that it becomes a natural part of daily family life. Challenging as it is, with some flexibility, creativity, and perseverance, perhaps your family can be one of that select 5 percent who have regular family devotions. Here are some guidelines to help you get started.

- *Find a Regular Time for Family Devotions.* This provides the benefit of an appointment the family members know about in advance and can plan for. It doesn't have to be a daily time, so long as it is a regular part of your family's life. If you can't manage a daily time, try for Monday, Wednesday, and Friday or even once or twice a week. If your weekday schedule is impossible, you may want to schedule some or all of your family devotions on weekends.
- *Find a Time When All the Family Can Be Together.* Often, mealtimes are the best time, especially if you're able to eat together on a regular basis. But if mealtimes don't work, here's where the creativity and flexibility come in.

  For some years when our sons were younger, we had our daily devotions at breakfast. Perhaps you can meet early (or late, after homework) in the evening. The time of day is not as important as finding a time when everyone can be there.
- *Be Creative and Have Fun.* David Veerman, author of *Serious Fun* and *More Serious Fun,*[9] suggests asking the children to act out Bible stories or relevant incidents in their lives. It will help keep them interested and involved so they learn more effectively. Use the "parent lecture method" sparingly. Rotate leadership among family members as they are willing and able. Our children can teach us if we let them.

Remember that the purpose of family devotions is not just to provide another opportunity for Mom or Dad to lecture. Some of that is necessary and good, but a steady diet will kill family devotions. Set a goal of having everyone participate to the extent of his ability. Let the children choose songs and lead them. Some will be able to read part of the lesson. Others may want to pray.

If you sing, incorporate songs from camp or Sunday school. And don't forget to have fun. That's the special privilege of childhood. Plan a simple game or something you know your children will enjoy. David danced before the Lord. Surely you can play a game and have a little fun.

Be flexible enough to change direction if necessary. If one family member comes to the group with a special problem or question, that may be just the time to drop the prepared lesson and discuss how God and God's Word can help.[10]

- *Use the Tried and True "KISS" Method.* I heard two preschoolers arguing loudly one day. "Jesus died for *me*," one said. "No, He died for me," said the other. And so the argument went. It made perfect sense to each that if the Sunday school teacher told them, "Jesus died for you," that's what it meant: He died for "me" and not anyone else!

Young children think literally and concretely. The doctrine of the "vicarious atonement" of Christ (the understanding that Christ died in my place as payment for my sins) is an abstract and difficult idea for a child to understand. So be sensitive to the language you use in your family devotions, especially with the youngest children. But don't neglect to teach something just because it may be difficult or confusing. Try to get material that is "age appropriate" for your children. If what you're using isn't well suited to your children's understanding, experiment with other material. Try your best to keep the language as simple, clear, and concrete as possible. That's the essence of the KISS method: Keep It Short and Simple.

• *Make Your Lessons Practical and Concrete.* At least once, you've probably come away from a church service feeling frustrated. "I spent twenty-five minutes listening to that sermon and heard absolutely nothing that I can apply in my life." You knew you deserved and needed better. So do children. They also experience frustration after listening to lessons that seem to have no relation to their lives, that offer no answers to the questions they're asking.

You know what's going on in your children's lives, and you know the problems they're facing, so try to show how the Word of God offers help, direction, and encouragement. Help them see and marvel at how God's Word has something to say to four or five-year-olds, ten-year-olds, and teens. It is very important to a child that you "demonstrate the practicality of Christianity" to his life. If you don't, "as he grows older, he may reject sacred ideas as being impractical to his secular world."[11]

Issues facing your family may be the source of discussion for some weeks. Or maybe you'll want to ask each family member to suggest one question he or she has about God's Word. This helps keep devotions in touch with the lives of our children as well as with the wisdom of God's Word.

Don't hesitate to share stories of God at work in your own life. Your children love to hear them, and they will learn from them too. Offer concrete, practical examples. Share your faith with your children so that their faith can grow as a result.

• *Prepare in Advance.* Family devotions need not require great blocks of time to prepare (fifteen or twenty minutes may be sufficient), but they do need to be prepared in advance. That advance preparation includes regular prayer also. If more discussion during devotions is your goal, or if there is a problem you want to overcome, prepare one or two simple questions that can serve as discussion starters.

- *Don't Forget to Pray!* Prayer time during devotions doesn't have to be long and involved. With very young children, it probably shouldn't be. The language should be natural and simple. The most important thing is that you model prayer for your children. Prayer is the native language of the Christian. Encourage and invite (don't force) your children to pray. Your devotions will almost always suggest a theme for prayer, but ask the children if they have special concerns. You may want to keep a written journal of family prayers and a record of how God answers them. This has been a real "eye-opener" to many families.

The "Family Night"

In recent years, as regular family devotions have become harder to maintain under the increasing pressure of hectic family schedules, a new practice has gained popularity: the weekly "family night."

Did you ever notice that restaurants and movies often have special discounts on Monday and Tuesday evenings? Those are the nights of the week when people tend to go out the least. Perhaps one of those nights will present the least problems for getting the whole family together. But if those nights don't work, don't give up. Even the craziest family schedules yield at least one night when everyone can be there.

Choose your family night using some of the same guidelines that apply to family devotions. It's best to schedule a regular, weekly family night so that family members can count on it and plan it into their weekly schedules. Whenever a potential "conflict" arises, family members already know they have a prior commitment.

At the same time, be flexible. Activities such as school band concerts (and even work conflicts) often are scheduled far enough in advance so that, with planning, family nights can be worked around them. As children grow, family schedules change, so from time to time you may need to reexamine the best night for "family night."

Since family nights usually happen only once a week (sometimes less often), they usually involve more time than just the ten or fifteen minutes given to daily family devotions. A couple of hours provides enough time to really do some fun and rewarding things together. If you enjoy planning family time, you'll enjoy discovering all the things you can do together in a couple of hours. At the end of this chapter, I've listed some resources to help you get started.

For example, Robert Webber, a professor at Wheaton College in Illinois and author of *The Book of Family Prayer*, tells how his family sets aside one night each week for a weekly "meal service." The family's best dishes come out and a special dinner is prepared. After the meal, the family participates in a brief service of prayer and Scripture readings around the table.[12] Webber's book gives plenty of such "services" for weekly use and for special occasions such as Lent, Advent, Thanksgiving, birthdays, anniversaries, and just having friends over.

When our boys were younger, we held our weekly family night every Monday. By 7:00 P.M. we had finished the meal and adjourned to the family room to eat our dessert and watch the excellent PBS series for children called "Wonderworks." We really looked forward to this special time together each week.

Some families play games or work on special, fun projects together. They may also sing a hymn, read a Scripture, and pray. Dean and Grace Merrill's excellent book, *Together at Home: 100 Proven Ways to Nurture your Child's Faith*, delivers on the promise of its title and provides scores of enjoyable and meaningful ideas for your family-night activities.[13]

The keys to a successful family night are simple: advance planning; a consistent, regularly scheduled time; an element of fun; and a spiritual focus. And don't permit distractions: no visits from friends, and all telephone calls will be returned later.

A regular, weekly family night takes a relatively small investment of time but pays significant rewards. Like a good exercise program, a regular family night can build family strength, both spiritually and emotionally.

If you are convinced of the privilege and responsibility you have as a parent to pass on your faith to your children but are plagued by the suspicion that the clock is beating you and your family in this regard, don't give up! Family devotions work for some families; maybe they'll work for yours.

But for many families, a regular "family night" is just what they need. Perhaps now is the time to begin yours. Whichever approach you choose, the success of your family night and the payback for your family depends on what we'll discuss next: your family atmosphere.

CHAPTER SIX

_____

_____

_____

Your Family Atmosphere: Watch My Lips or Watch My Life

"**H**e's modeling after his grandfather and you," my wife said. She had just seen our teenage son give a dollar to his younger brother. There was no particular occasion that prompted this act. He just knew his younger brother would enjoy the extra money. So he gave it, just as his father and grandfather had done to him many times in the past.

The old cliché is true. The faith, values, and actions that our children develop at home are as much caught as taught. That's why the "family atmosphere" is so influential in affecting parents' ability to pass on their faith to their children.

Every family has a family atmosphere, whether they're aware of it or not. You don't have to go out and buy a design and then spend months building one (although, as we'll see, it may need some major repairs). It's already there. It's that big bundle of experiences that your family shares together every day: meals, homework, discussions (and arguments!), prayers, fun, illnesses, hugs—the list is endless.

Your family atmosphere is the emotional and spiritual "soil" in which your children grow and develop. If that soil is rich in the nutrients of love, kindness, and spiritual sensitivity, your children have a head start at growing up to be self-confident, loving, kind, and spiritually sensitive adults. If those nutrients are rare in your family atmosphere, your children's emotional and spiritual growth may be stunted.

Of the different approaches to nurturing our children's faith, which one is most likely to pay the greatest rewards for the time invested—family devotions, family night, or family atmosphere?

You've probably already guessed my answer, but it's important to say it again: all three approaches have much to offer families. Children need to see their parents read, study, and revere the Scriptures if they are to learn to do the same. They need to see and hear their parents pray if they are to accept the centrality of prayer in the life of faith and even learn how to pray.

As busy as many of us are, a regular family night is a great way for families to celebrate their bonds of love and deepen their faith. It may be just the answer that many hurried, harried families seek.

However, the effectiveness of these two nurturing approaches depends on the quality of the family atmosphere. The positive effects of regular family devotions or a family night are greatly multiplied by a spiritually rich family atmosphere.

A combination of all three of these approaches would be tremendously powerful. But here's where I make another confession. We've tried both family devotions and family nights with our family. Each worked for a time, and I'm glad we did them. I wish we could have been more successful, especially at regular devotions. But, as our family grew and changed, it seemed that we needed to adapt to those changes. In recent years, we've come to rely almost exclusively on the family atmosphere approach.

Watch My Life

The idea of the life-shaping power of the family atmosphere is nothing new. It's at least as old as Moses' instructions to the families of Israel as recorded in the book of Deuteronomy. Moses begins by telling parents to develop their own relationship to God. "Love the LORD *your* God with all *your* heart and with all *your* soul and with all *your* strength. These commandments that I give you today are to be upon *your* hearts."[1]

Then, after being certain of their own relationship with the Lord, parents were told to teach God's commandments to their children. They were to "press" the commandments on their children so that they left their mark on the children's hearts.

Notice how Moses instructed parents to do this. No doubt, some formal teaching was involved, but Moses didn't even mention it here. He didn't say "Be sure your children get to their classes in the faith education tent regularly" or "Be sure you spend at least fifteen minutes daily reading the Scriptures with them." I'm sure Moses took it for granted that instruction in the faith would take place in some form.

But what Moses *did* say indicates how important the family atmosphere is to a child's growing faith. Moses made it clear that this is the most essential, most fundamental area in which parents could focus their efforts. That hasn't changed.

"Talk about them [God's commandments] when you sit at home and when you walk along the road and when you lie down and when you get up," Moses said.[2] In other words, use the everyday experiences of family life to train your children in faith and godly living.

My father helped me see how to do this when he and my mother visited a few years ago. For as long as I can remember, my dad, a dairy farmer, has always (I mean, *every day*) gone out for breakfast after the morning chores are finished. He'll clean up and drive to a local coffee shop. It's part of his social life, and perhaps a reward for getting up at 3:45 A.M. each morning!

So when he and Mom come to visit, he and I and my two sons go out for breakfast. It's just taken for granted. It's a morning ritual that we "men" all enjoy.

One foggy Saturday morning we drove a few miles to a local restaurant for breakfast. Because of the fog, I had put my car lights on. You guessed it! I left them on all through breakfast, and when we returned the car battery was dead.

Since we had brought our small car with a standard transmission, we thought we could push it down the slight grade in the parking lot and start it. But neither Dad nor I are very mechanically inclined. We pushed and pushed and still the car wouldn't start.

We were about to give up and call my wife to rescue us when out of the restaurant came a man who offered to help us. He knew exactly what to do and with one good push the car started. As we drove out of the parking lot toward home, Dad said, "Wasn't God good to send us that man to help us!" We all nodded in agreement.

"Wasn't God good . . ." How easy a thing to say right then! How appropriate! But *I* hadn't said it. If Dad hadn't, an opportunity to recognize and give thanks for God's care and His activity in our family's life would have been lost. I was grateful to Dad for those words. They taught us all an important lesson.

Moses said, "Talk with your children about the things of God in the everyday experiences of life." That means we should talk with our children "about what is important to us when we're in the car together, when we're in the yard, when we're in the home with the TV off, at mealtimes, and at bedtimes."[3] This is the best way to open their hearts and minds to see and experience God's presence and care in their everyday lives.

Practicing the Presence of God

What is it that has most shaped your life and relationship to God? It's probably some person or group of people—perhaps your parents, or a Sunday school or youth worker, or your church fellowship. Information is important to the growth of our children's faith, but information alone rarely shapes lives. Rather, people shape lives, especially children's lives. Children are shaped by those people who love them and care for them and whom they can love in return. Most of the time, these people are a child's parents.

It's not hard for our children to love us. We're there for them and with them, actively and visibly caring for them daily. But how can we help them come to love Jesus (whom they can't see)? How can we shape our family's atmosphere so that our children come to love Him as we do?

The answer isn't necessarily found in any big, time-consuming projects or programs. It is found in using the daily life of the home to help our children see and experience the active love and care of Jesus in their lives.

In the seventeenth century a monk named Brother Lawrence wrote a book called *Practicing the Presence of God*. It has since become a classic of Christian literature. In it, Brother Lawrence relates his desire to sense God's continual presence in his daily life, whether he was cooking in the monastery kitchen or praying with the other monks. All times of the day, all activities of his life were the same to him: opportunities to commune with God, be in His presence, and experience His care. He called this "practicing the presence of God."

I believe this should be our goal as Christian parents: by our family atmosphere, help our children practice the presence of God daily.

How do we create this kind of family atmosphere that practices the presence of God? We pray as a family when family finances are a problem, when someone is struggling in school, when someone is sick, or a parent's job is especially stressful. A petition included with thanks before a meal or during bedtime prayers isn't very time consuming. It does teach, however, that we believe God is with us, cares about our situation, and can be called upon to help. This also provides an opportunity for our children to see and experience God's answers to their prayers. And when those prayers are answered, don't forget to thank Him. That teaches our children the proper response to God's presence and care. Just as we teach them good social manners, we teach them good "spiritual manners."

Without taking any time to plan or manufacture them, every family has many experiences every day that parents can use to lead their children "to reach out to Jesus and run to him. There may be times of sorrow, of sins, of some particular hurt, or of some sudden movement of love in the children's heart. At these moments, attentive parents can lead their children to speak to Jesus and to listen to him, to rely on him, to receive from him, to embrace him."[4]

If we are aware of these moments, we can open our children's hearts and minds to the presence of God. These are very special times when our children meet and experience Christ personally and come to know and love him "as Savior, forgiver, healer, leader, comforter, protector, and God."[5]

It's not hard to help our children practice the presence of God in their lives. Opportunities abound in daily family life. But we may need to sharpen our own spiritual vision. We may need to practice the presence of God in our own lives first. As we spend regular time with

God in daily prayer, in reading His Word, and in corporate worship, our own eyes will be opened to see Him with us. Then we can show Him to our children.

Educators tell us that the people who have the greatest impact on children are those with whom the children have a consistent, loving, long-term relationship. The impact is greater if our children are exposed to these people in a wide variety of life's experiences. (Sounds like a description of a parent, doesn't it?) Within that long-term, loving relationship, our children "take after" us and model our behavior and attitudes (as in the case of my teenage son giving a dollar to his younger brother).

If you're like I am, you may need to be much more verbal, in a natural way, about your faith in front of your children. Some of us are not comfortable with that. It may not be easy for us to pray with others. But inside the home, we need to put aside our inhibitions as much as possible. Our children need to hear us talk about our relationship with Jesus and what He's doing in our lives. They need to see that "their parents' relationship with Jesus is as real and important as the relationship they have with Grandpa and Grandma, coworkers, neighbors, and friends."[6]

Children are great imitators and great responders. They learn by watching and then imitating (the formal term is *modeling*). If we say, for example, that the Bible is the most important book in the world, but they rarely see us read it, what conclusion will they draw? If we tell them it's important to pray, but they never see us do it, what conclusion will they draw?

But if we let them see us recognize and respond to God's presence in our lives (as my father did when the car battery was dead), they will learn to do it, too. In a real sense, loving and following Jesus becomes as natural as loving and following Mom and Dad. It becomes an essential part of their self-identity as members of the family.[7] And remember, we didn't talk about any time-consuming program here; just using the life experiences that already come your family's way.

When my family lived in Pittsburgh, we lived in an older house in a Jewish section of the city. We soon discovered that every house on the block (including our own) had a *mezuzah* on the door frame. That is a tiny cannister containing a miniature copy of the Torah, the first five books of the Old Testament.

It didn't take long to figure out why it was there. Referring to the things of God, Moses told the parents of Israel to "Tie them as symbols on your hands and bind them on your foreheads. Write them on the doorframes of your houses and on your gates."[8] Orthodox Jews take those commands literally, even today, so every house on our street had the commandments of God on the door frames.

Here again, Moses was talking about the family atmosphere. Christian symbols, art, and music have an important place in our homes. By themselves, they have little effect, but together with the example we parents provide, they help to shape and reinforce the rich, spiritual atmosphere of the home. They serve as tangible reminders, both to us and our children, of just who we are and what we believe as a family.

"There's No Time Like the Present"

It's never too early (or too late) to begin shaping and reshaping your family atmosphere. We talked with our children about Jesus from their earliest days. Like many families, we sang lullabies such as "Jesus Loves the Little Children" and "Jesus Loves Me This I Know" while we rocked and fed them. As they grew, it was natural for them to speak of Him, think about Him throughout daily life, and talk with Him.

Starting early helps our children become aware of Jesus in their lives early on. Then, their awareness of Him can grow and develop as they do, through all the stages of their lives. A real and growing relationship with Jesus Christ is not just for adults.

"Turning to Christ, conversing with Him in prayer, accepting His love and loving Him in return are for youngsters, too. The fact that a child's relationship with Jesus may be immature does not mean that it is not real. Surely the relationship of a child with Jesus will have to grow and develop as a child grows, but there is no reason why it should not start when the child is very young."[9]

But no matter what age your children are, there's no time like the present to begin shaping your family atmosphere to nurture their faith. If your children are older, don't let that stop you. God can still work great things in them as they see what He has done in you. If your children aren't born yet, it's still not too early to begin because the place to begin is always with you!

It's not easy being a Christian parent. We are called to put our faith right out there where our children can see it and imitate it. In a very real sense we share our own faith with our children so that they too may have faith. It is, after all, "in the atmosphere of their parents' faith [that] their own faith is born".[10] So work on deepening your own faith and relationship to God. Then, expose that faith to your children so that they, too, can "taste and see that the LORD is good."[11]

If you're someone who already practices a daily time of meeting God in Bible reading and prayer (ten to fifteen minutes is plenty for a start) and weekly worship, you're already a long way down the road to creating a spiritually rich family atmosphere. You may not need to invest much additional time. All you may need is some sharpening of your own spiritual senses so that you can share your faith with your children.

On the other hand, if you find that you need to invest some time in yourself in order to enrich your family atmosphere, just start with what's managable for you and grow as you can. Remember small, regular investments yield great returns for your family. That's the way to beat the clock and experience the great satisfaction of nurturing the growing faith of your children.

RESOURCES:

Here is a sampling of resources with which I am personally familiar. They can help you beat the clock in your effort to pass on your faith to your children.

Personal Devotional Material:

Adults:	Discovery
	Encounter With God
	(Advanced Series)
Older Teens:	AM/PM
Pre-teens or Young Teens:	One to One
Elementary (2nd-5th gr.):	Quest
Pre-schoolers:	Find Out (5-6 yrs.)
	Simon and Sarah

Most of these are published in quarterly booklets. All are available from Scripture Union, 7000 Ludlow Street, Philadelphia., PA 19082.

Family Nights:

Christian Family Activities by Wayne Rickerson (Standard)

Together at Home: 100 Proven Ways to Nurture your Children's Faith by Dean and Grace Merrill (Thomas Nelson)

Time for the Family (3 Vols.) (Scripture Union)

Serious Fun and *More Serious Fun* by David Veerman (Victor Books)

Family Atmosphere:

The Book of Family Prayer by Robert E. Webber (Thomas Nelson)

Building Your Child's Faith by Alice Chapin (Here's Life Publishers)

Helping Your Children Know Jesus by Larry Richards (Standard)

CHAPTER SEVEN

Family Rituals and Traditions: Making Memories, Growing Hope

Every bedtime ended the same way on Walton's Mountain. One by one, the lights went out; first in the children's rooms and then in the parents'. One by one, everyone wished each other "good night." That was the Walton family ritual for ending the day.

Even though we knew they were only a "television family," they were still a very special one. They were clearly a close-knit, warm, and loving family, just like we all wanted to be. And it was obvious they had many family rituals and traditions.

To some folks, mention of family rituals and traditions brings to mind painfully boring family activities that everyone had to do but no one enjoyed. Perhaps it was the holiday visit to great-grandmother's house. It seemed the parents spent all their time trying to keep the children from breaking everything while the children spent all their time fighting with each other because they were frustrated and bored.

To others, however, talk of traditions and rituals evokes different memories, more like the Waltons' "good night." They remember the fun of decorating the Christmas tree together on the first day of Advent or the special birthday meal that meant you could have anything for dinner you wanted, even all desserts! Sometimes the memories are of simpler things, such as mealtimes together or bedtime stories and prayers.

My wife remembers vividly the Saturday night ritual in her family when she was growing up. Every Saturday after dinner, each of the five children would take a bath to get ready for church the next day. While the children took their baths, her father would shine everyone's shoes.

Good memories or bad, we can't forget those family rituals and traditions. They're part of us forever. We often go to great pains to share the special ones with our own children so they can experience the same warmth and specialness those family rituals and traditions gave to us.

The frustration comes when we discover that implementing and enjoying family rituals and traditions takes time and effort.

Routine or Ritual?

Paul Pearsall, author of *The Power of the Family*, says that in many families today, each member lives in his "own unique time zone." As a result, the lives of family members are never quite in "sync." They don't quite mesh.[1]

Much of what we do every day—getting up, eating, relaxing, sleeping, doing chores—is routine. We go through our routines to get them over with so that we can get on with our individual "agendas," the things that are "the real business of living": work, school, leisure. The contest between the clock and family life means that we must be sure that this healthy part of family living—rituals and traditions—is not gradually "squeezed out" of our family life.[2]

To do that, Pearsall recommends consciously trying to see much of what we do (feeding the kids, getting them into bed, washing the dishes) not as an obligation or chore to be "gotten over with," but as an opportunity for a family ritual.[3]

While routines are designed for getting over with, Pearsall says, rituals (even simple ones such as holding hands around the dinner table to pray before meals) are designed for getting "with" family life and for strengthening family ties. In sharp contrast to deadly family routines, family rituals celebrate togetherness and focus on sharing and enjoying the many things families do together.[4]

Rituals force us to slow down just a bit. "Routines are done quickly, automatically, and without much thought. Rituals, by contrast, are done slowly, intensely, and contemplatively."[5] Bedtime rituals, sharing reports of the day around the dinner table, family prayers, and doing chores together can become family rituals that represent "the tangible acting out of the shared belief that *even ordinary family activities are meaningful and significant in their own right* (emphasis mine)." [6] They transform our family routines (dare I say even redeem them) allowing us to really experience and celebrate family living.

Chances are that every Sunday in church the order of worship follows a ritual that is much the same from week to week. That can become a "worship routine" that is dry and unrewarding. On the other hand, the ritual can free and assist us to experience the sacredness of worship. In the same way, family rituals enable us to experience some of the sacredness of family life.

Life *can* be done hurriedly and individually, but family life should be shared and savored slowly. Family rituals help us to slow down and "smell the roses." Maybe you are becoming convinced of that, pressure from the clock or not! But there are even more wonderful ways that family rituals and traditions help us. We'll look at some of those now.

Who We Are and Whose We Are

One of the "big events" of my childhood was going bowling with my family. During the fall and winter months, our family and two or three others went bowling just about every Friday night for years. There were just two lanes and they weren't automatic. My dad would hire neighborhood boys to be our "pin setters."

The setting was primitive by today's standards, but we sure had fun! It didn't matter that the bowling balls seemed awfully heavy or that my score was never very good. This was more than just something the family did on Friday evenings. For those few hours, I could almost believe I was an adult, an "equal" with the rest. I was treated as a valued member of one of the bowling teams (though my score never justified that).

Bowling was something we Pattersons did together as a family. It was one of our family rituals. For some years after we had left home, whenever we got together with our folks, one of us could be counted on to say, "Let's go bowling."

That's another of the special benefits of family rituals. They offer a concrete way to say, "I love you. I like being with you. I want to reenact what's important in life with you because you are important to me."[7] Our family rituals symbolize and express for us who we are as a family and the nature of our relationship together. For the Pattersons, Friday night bowling helped define us as a family who enjoyed being together and took time to have fun.

Our faith rituals play the same important role in defining our identity as a family of faith. Rituals built around regular church attendance and celebration of the great feasts of the church year (the birth of Christ, His Resurrection, Pentecost, etc.) identify us as people committed to honoring Christ. These same rituals symbolize and teach our children about our family identity in a nonverbal but clear way long before they are able to understand or explain these rituals. They are an important part of the family atmosphere discussed in the previous chapter.

Our family is the first and most important place where we "belong." It's the one place where, as the poet Robert Frost put it, "when you have to go there, they have to take you in." Family traditions—a rented movie on Friday night, Thanksgiving at the grandparents, Advent calendars, and a Christmas Eve "watch night" service—help build the sense that we belong to a special, unique group called "our family."

Family vacations are another way to build that sense of belonging and identity. They provide a special time to be together for an extended period and do things the family has planned and anticipated all year long. In other words, they offer times to "do" vacation traditions.

For the past twelve years we have taken our family vacation on Nantucket, a small, beautiful gem of an island off the coast of Massachusetts. It's probably no surprise that Nantucket in August is one of our more popular family traditions. We enjoy going to the beach, exploring the island, and going into the lovely little town in the evening.

While we're there, we have plenty of time to do things on our own, but we spend a lot of relaxed time together. By the time the two weeks are up, our teenage son is likely to say something like "Enough of this family togetherness for awhile, Dad!"

Families who lack a sense of closeness often don't take the time to build family rituals and traditions. Family specialist Dolores Curran observes that "families who treasure their traditions and rituals seem automatically to have a sense of family. Traditions are the underpinning in such families, regarded as necessities, not frills.

If there's a conflict between a tradition and a responsibility, the tradition usually wins."[8]

Celebrating birthdays, eating together, praying together, family vacations, and countless other family traditions and rituals all take time and effort to carry out. But to the families that invest that time and effort, they've become essential to their sense of closeness and belonging.

Traditions That Bind

Did you belong to a "club" when you were a child? I can remember at least two that I was a part of. Children love clubs. They thrive on a sense of belonging to a special, unique group that is distinguishable from all others.[9] The first and most important club they belong to is, of course, their family. As we have seen, rituals and traditions help build that sense of belonging.

If a family is "under-ritualized," caught up in getting through life instead of spending time celebrating and sharing life together, children may not feel that sense of belonging that they so want and need. They may begin to look elsewhere to find a "family" to belong to. That "somewhere else" may turn out to be an unhealthy peer group or even a gang.

Psychiatrist Dr. Paul Pearsall says that his research with adolescent boys who have joined gangs indicates these boys usually come from homes lacking a system of family rituals. The gang rituals, then, become substitutes for the missing family rituals. They fill, at least temporarily, the need of gang members for predictability and control, as well as for significance, order, and a meaningful life.[10]

Pearsall suggests that maybe these boys aren't just "rebellious." "Maybe we are mistaking adolescent rebelliousness for our own unconscious exclusion and neglect of our developing young people. If we don't have time to do things with them, to ritualize their daily life with us, they will find others who will. Drug use, alchoholism and the sometimes general disregard for the value of life shown by the senseless risks our young people occasionally take may be a symptom of the lack of the consistency of ritual. . . . All of adolescence in the United States may be seen as a mass cultural ritual evolving to fill the void of intimate family rituals."[11]

Mealtimes together, family worship, ice cream on Sunday evening or pancakes on Saturday morning, family vacations, and other such rituals and traditions are more than just "fun." They give our children a sense of significance as well as security in life's predictability and order.

Family rituals and traditions not only foster a sense of belonging (a sense of whose we are) but they "give us a way to come together and define who we are as a family"[12] (a sense of who we are). One family I know has a tradition of helping to serve the homeless at a shelter one night each month. That reminds them of their identity as a Christian family who wants to serve "the least of these My brethren."[13]

Family reunions are a tradition that affirms and celebrates our family identity. Alex Haley, author of the best seller *Roots*, calls family reunions "the conveyor belts of our individual histories. They reaffirm the thread of continuity, establish pride in self and kin and transmit a family's awareness of itself from the youngest to the oldest."[14]

The Patterson family reunion is held every summer at my parents' farm in upstate New York. Anywhere from forty-five to sixty people come, some from as far away as California and Florida. They come in all ages and stages of life.

It's always quite an experience. We gather for a whole day at a nearby lake. We mostly eat and talk (there's quite a bit of both). I try to arrange for our family to attend as regularly as possible. It's the only time we see some of those aunts and uncles and cousins, and I want my children to know them as members of their extended family, not just "mere names on a Christmas card."[15]

Dad's farm is the source of another summer family tradition. For at least the past fifteen summers, Dad has planted two or three acres of land near the house with sweet corn. That small plot of sweet corn is dwarfed by the tens of acres of field corn growing nearby, but it is the sweet corn that gets all the attention.

The sweet corn is usually ripe in mid to late August. Dad hires local youth to help pick it, and then he sells it to the local folks and the many summer residents of the area. It's famous for its taste and priced at a bargain. One of our family traditions is to visit the farm for a couple of days just in time to help harvest—and devour—that delicious corn. When Mom asks, "Are you coming for corn?" we all know just what she means.

Our boys enjoy helping their grandfather pick and sell the corn, and we all enjoy eating it. Their grandmother freezes large quaties that we'll get to enjoy all winter. Corn is a tradition that is just part of being a Patterson. It's one more link in a strong chain of traditions that stretches across the generations and helps bind our children to their grandparents. That, too, is a very special gift of family traditions: binding one generation to another.[16]

Celebrating the Special within the Ordinary

Rituals also enable us, as one observer put it, to celebrate "the special within the ordinary" of daily family living.[17] They help us mark off and celebrate special family times like birthdays, anniversaries, and holidays. But they also enable us to celebrate transition times such as graduations, promotions, or even the daily transitions of bedtime or going to day-care.

In chapter two, we saw how the daily routine of a young child's bedtime can become an affirming and comforting ritual. A warm bath, a Bible story, bedtime prayers, and a goodnight kiss can lift the transition from waking time to sleep (with all the fears of what will happen when the lights go out and Mom and Dad leave) out of the routine and ordinary into the special by making it a reminder of the love, security, and stability of the child's family.

For many families, there is another ordinary, daily transition that could stand a big dose of "specialness": leaving our children at their place of day-care. Some parents smooth this transition with a daily discussion of the child's activities in the day ahead. "Tell me what you think you'll do today" or "Let's see if I can guess what you'll do today." "I'll be thinking of you when you're doing those things. I'll probably be doing . . . Will you try to think about me, too?" Then a hug and a kiss marks the end of the ritual.

All of this can be just a routine you go through in order to get your child to let you leave with a minimum of tears. But it can also become a ritual that binds you and your child close throughout the day and eases the pain as you part at the day-care door. A daily ritual such as a special story or game when you arrive home each day makes this end-of-the-day transition something special, too.

Most of the time, family mealtimes are about as ordinary as you can get. Holding hands around the table as you pray before eating, having each member tell one thing (good or bad) about their day, or having a "favorite meal" night for one family member each week are simple rituals that lift ordinary mealtimes into the realm of the special. They help us celebrate the fact that family members belong together, care about each other, and "feed" each other as they gather around the family table.

Jewish families who celebrate the Sabbath meal around the table on Friday evenings use this ordinary family routine to strengthen and enrich their families. The worship ritual they incorporate into their mealtime affirms, at least once a week, the family's deepest shared identity and values. It lifts that weekly meal out of the realm of the ordinary.

What a wise way to beat the clock! Most of the rituals we've discussed, especially those associated with eating and sleeping, don't require any extra investment of our limited time. "Everyone has to sleep and eat anyway, so the only change is to ritualize and share these activities as a family."[18]

Family specialist Dolores Curran tells of one special tradition observed in her family. Once a year she and her son schedule one entire day together that they call "our day." On that much anticipated day they go out together and do whatever they want.[19]

An entire day together is great, but we will want to find smaller snatches of time to spend with our children throughout the year too. Spending just fifteen minutes a day with each child is a very special way to celebrate the love of parent and child and keep communication lines open.

Some families schedule a monthly "date" between each parent and child. It might be nothing more than an hour or two at the local fast-food restaurant or a museum, but they do it regularly and they do it together. It *is* an investment of time, but it pays big dividends.

Linking Faith and Family

When you think of some of the traditions your family observes that express your faith comitment, what comes to mind? Prayer before meals? A family night or devotion time? Serving meals for the homeless? Regular attendance at Sunday worship?

The rituals and traditions that express our family's faith come in all shapes and sizes. Whether large or small, they remind us that "faith and family life belong together and family traditions are one way to link everyone in the family together in that faith."[20]

Dolores Curran rightly emphasizes the importance of investing time in family faith rituals and traditions. She observes that it is "a great tragedy that we have allowed religion to become a subject to be taught rather than a belief to be ritualized in our daily lives. Faith is rarely passed on because of nuances in doctrine or theology. It is passed on because of the difference it makes in daily life. The best way of experiencing this difference is through traditions and rituals."[21]

As followers of Christ, one of the beliefs my wife and I want to shape in our children is service to the poor. Our family is probably not too different from yours. We live in a comfortable middle-class neighborhood, and our children go to a nice, suburban school. Like you, we lead busy lives. My wife and I struggle with how to help our children develop and maintain a heart of caring and service to those in need.

Even busy families can develop family traditions that help proclaim and pass on this important element of faith. Almost any family can find a few hours once a month to work at a church food pantry where folks in need are treated with dignity and offered help in Christ's name.

Our family stumbled on such a way almost by accident. When we moved to a new city, my wife took a teaching position at an inner city school just two blocks from the City Mission. One day she heard that the Mission needed volunteers to help serve a meal on Christmas Day, so we went and helped serve that meal. Christmas at the City Mission soon became a Patterson family tradition.

Our next step was to call the Mission and ask if we could come and serve a meal once a month. That tradition keeps us in touch with the needs of others and allows us to serve them together, as followers of Christ. It's a tradition I'd be pleased to have my children pass on to their children.

Of course, the needy require our care throughout the year, but the holidays lend themselves especially well to establishing family traditions of care and service. Your family is never too young to start. "Young children ought to see their parents volunteering to drop off books at a pediatric ward or give clothes to the needy. Later on, the kids can participate in some small way, perhaps willingly foregoing one of their own [Christmas] gifts to spend the money on someone less privileged. The spirit of giving should be as strong a tradition as the joy of receiving."[22]

Susan Abel Lieberman, in her warm and practical book, *New Traditions*,[23] uncovers many valuable, holiday-related traditions. Some are familiar, some are not. For example, she tells of Christian families who celebrate Christmas as "Jesus' Birthday." They have a real party with a birthday cake and sing "Happy Birthday" to Jesus. That tradition helps at least one family keep focused on "the true meaning of Christmas."[24]

She also tells of a Jewish family who observes a "Gift of Self" night during the celebration of the eight days of Hannukah. On that night, each family member is required to give a gift of themselves to another family member or to the entire family. Now that's a tradition Christian families could enthusiastically adopt.[25]

But family life is mostly lived in that vast expanse of time we call "every day," not just in the great faith festivals. It's true that "families are woven together slowly and gradually—not just during the holidays and other special occasions."[26] And there are wonderful family traditions that celebrate our faith without any link to a holiday or Christian festival.

For as long as their children were at home, one family observed the tradition of celebrating the baptismal anniversary of each of their children as well as their birthdays.[27] This tradition could be adopted to celebrate their confirmation date or the date of their profession of faith. All the rituals and traditions we've discussed—daily

prayers, family mealtimes, bedtime, worship, and service—link our families and our faith together in a seam-
less and beautiful garment that is a blessed heritage for
our children.

New Families Need Traditions Too!

Rituals and traditions act as the "shock absorbers" of
family life. They help smooth out the many bumps in
the road that every family navigates.

Some years ago, our family moved to a new home in
upstate New York after living for fifteen years in Pittsburgh. Both of our boys were born in Pittsburgh. It was
the only home our family knew.

We had developed many family traditions over those
years in Pittsburgh: family camping over the Memorial
Day and Labor Day holidays, going to "Fort Ligonier
Days" (a celebration of Revolutionary War history) over
the Columbus Day holiday, visiting the stores down-
town at the opening of the Christmas shopping season,
and many others. Most of those traditions were tied to
the western Pennsylvania area. When we moved, we left
them behind.

There was one tradition that helped us tremendously
in those first few months when we were cut off from
friends and familiar places: regular attendance at public
worship. Right away we had new friends, a new family.
We weren't strangers for long.

There were other traditions that made the move with
us to New York. We still went fishing together. We still
rented a movie on Friday evening. All the traditions we
brought with us helped us over the sometimes "bumpy"
transition to life in a new area. They reminded us that
though our surroundings were new, some important

things hadn't changed. We were still a family, still the Pattersons, still in control of our family life.

Of course, we developed some new traditions to replace the ones left behind. Now we could make monthly visits to my parents' farm or the nearby lakeside camp owned by my wife's parents. The camp became a new place for our family to enjoy Memorial Day and Labor Day (and a lot of other days).

We started a new tradition of buying and decorating our Christmas tree on the first day of Advent. And thanks to my youngest son, we also developed a new Sunday ritual: stopping on the way home from church to buy (and devour) a large bag of potato chips!

Our family's experience was not that unusual. In this mobile society of ours, many families move every year. But for every family that moves geographically, there's one that "moves" in another way. They don't move to a new area, but they do become a new family. This "move" often represents an even harder transition.

Think about the families in your neighborhood or your church. Chances are some of them are two parent families with their own biological children living in the home. But the chances are that there are many other, newer types of families there, also. There are single parent families resulting from death or divorce and there are also step-families and blended families.

These newer kinds of families need their own rituals and traditions for the same reasons other families do: for warmth and closeness, a sense of identity, and a means of celebration and affirmation of family faith and values. But they need them even more.

The loss of a parent or a spouse through death or divorce is never easy. Rituals and traditions can help ease the way for both single parents and their children.

In the case of the death of a spouse, "doing it just the way Dad did it" becomes a ritual that may bring a sense of stability and comfort to children. Other times, a new tradition or ritual will help to reflect and celebrate the new family situation. The important thing (as with all family traditions) is that everyone—parent and child—agree on what and how to celebrate their new situation.

Single Parents Can Have Them Too!

Time, money, and support: these are the biggest problems that face parents, especially single parents. They need to develop their own special traditions and rituals to meet the challenges of single parenting. For example, one single mother has a nightly ritual of thirty minutes alone in the bath after work to soak, relax, and enjoy the quiet. Only after being renewed by this nightly ritual does she begin preparing dinner.

Susan Lieberman gives examples of some traditions and rituals that single parents have developed to help them cope with and celebrate their situations. One is a clever variation on the nightly bedtime story ritual.

Maria, a working mom, is the mother of a four-year-old son. After a full day of work, she battles traffic to get to his day-care center before 6:00 P.M. By the time dinner is over and he has his bath, both mother and son are exhausted. Reading that bedtime story became a dreaded chore for Maria. So she invented "good morning stories." Just before bed, Maria and her son pick out a book to read in the morning. After they are dressed and breakfast is ready, they read it together. She is convinced they both enjoy the ritual "bedtime story" much more in the morning![28]

Lieberman also tells of a group of single moms who were determined to celebrate Mother's Day. These four single moms have established their own tradition of a Mother's Day Brunch. They draw names to buy presents for each other and they help each others' children buy Mother's Day presents. When the day arrives, they hire a sitter for their children and enjoy a sumptuous brunch while opening their presents. It's become one of their most treasured traditions.[29]

I admire the way one single parent copes with the feeling of "never having enough time" with her boys. She especially wanted to find time to spend with each boy individually. So she established the tradition of "Wednesday Morning Pancakes." Each Wednesday she drops one boy at school early and takes the other out to breakfast at a local pancake house.[30] This assures them of some special time together, and it "beats the clock" by doing something they'd do anyway—eat!

These are just a few examples of the creative ways single parents form new traditions and rituals. Although these few examples featured women, men could use them just as well. (How about a Father's Day Brunch?)

Family rituals and traditions must grow and change as our families grow and change. Forming new rituals and traditions reflects and celebrates those changes. In a similar way, maintaining some of the older ones enables us to celebrate who we have remained and what we have valued as a family through all the transitions of life.

Our rituals and traditions help our families sink roots deep in the soil of closeness and intimacy while giving us confidence in the future. They create memories that endure for a lifetime.

In those memories, grow the seeds of hope. It was never more true that "Hope is what we need so badly, and hope is based in memory. Rituals do much to feed that hope through memory. And hope is the travel virtue. It gets us from yesterday into today and gives us the courage to face tomorrow."[31]

What better time can we spend with our families than time that builds hope and faith and love? These three things—like our family rituals and traditions—endure forever.

CHAPTER EIGHT

Family Fun Without Guilt!

In his book *The Effective Father*, Gordon MacDonald tells how James Boswell, the biographer of Samuel Johnson, referred to a special day in his childhood when his father took him fishing. Even as an adult, Boswell remembered that fishing trip vividly. He often reflected on all that his father had taught him that day. It must have been a thoroughly enjoyable experience for that young boy.

MacDonald says that because Boswell mentioned the fishing trip so often, someone decided to check the journal Boswell's father kept in order to see what he had thought of that day so memorable to his son. The journal entry had only one sentence: "Gone fishing today with my son; a day wasted."[1]

"A day wasted." It's not easy to shake the belief, rooted in the modern work ethic, that work is sacred and fun is frivolous, that work is what's really significant in life. In addition, fun can seem not only frivolous but expensive, and we have neither time nor money to waste.[2]

Let me say it as clearly as I can: having fun together as a family *is* important. It *is* serious business. As with all of the activities we've discusssed in our effort to beat the clock, family fun yields great rewards to the family that invests even small amounts of time in it. Let's look at some of the reasons why this is true.

First, having fun together is good for all members of the family. It's no news that we adults need to relax, to play and have fun. By refreshing our spirits and renewing our bodies, play and fun become true sources of "re-creation." Play and fun are also great stress relievers—and who of us doesn't need that?

With just a little recreation and fun, we're much better equipped, emotionally and physically, to be the kind of parents and marriage partners we want to be.

Let Us Play

Secondly, our children need to play and have fun too. Play is their work; their "natural form of expression."[3] Through play, they work out their understanding of life: how to cooperate, get along with others, and win and lose graciously.

Through play, children learn to cope with their fears and worries.[4] There is so much we can help them learn and accomplish just by playing and having fun along-side them while sharing our insights and offering them our example.

Is your child taking a test in school this week? Is he entered in a competition soon? Is she new to the school or the neighborhood and still trying to make new friends and "fit in"? Then he or she needs to play and have fun (with you and with other children) to relieve stress.

Some children are under a great deal of stress. The stress is caused by family turmoil, by heavy academic pressures, and sometimes by having to carry what should be adult responsibilities. These and other stresses, which I discussed in my book *Brand-Name Kids: The Loss of Childhood in America*, [5] weigh heavily on children today.

The result of this stress is often restless, irritable children who seem tense or seriously depressed.[6] These children need help to recover a healthy, balanced life. Perhaps most of all, they need the permission of their parents to play and have fun.

One very good way to give them that permission is to play and have fun with them! Playing a board game with our children (and letting them win), dashing out for an unscheduled visit to the ice cream store, or getting down on the floor to wrestle helps put the "fun" and some much needed balance back into our children's lives. It says to them, "It's okay to take a break and have fun. It's important to play. Even adults do it." Play is an import-ant "stress-relief valve" for children just as it is for adults.

Play Builds Self-Esteem

Although Boswell's father didn't realize it, that "wasted day" fishing stayed with his son for a lifetime.

How important that boy must have felt having his dad all to himself for an entire day. That's another special gift we can give our children. By taking the time to play with them, we boost their self-esteem.

This is how one parent described the effect on her children when they spent some one-on-one time with their father. "Self-esteem blossomed as Dad took quality time to have fun with the child, to really listen without the competition that often comes from other siblings and even from another parent. It was a time for eye-balling the child and really finding out what was going on inside his head. It was a time from which a child could come away thinking 'Hey, I'm really important to Dad.'"[7] This parent talked mostly about having fun with Dad, but the same good effects come from time with Mom, too.

Now a word of caution about family fun time. If we play with our children for the sheer pleasure of being with them, everyone benefits. If, however, our body is there but our heart and mind are somewhere else, nobody benefits. That really is wasted time.

The third reward of family fun time is that it creates family memories. When our children were young we made it a tradition to go camping every Memorial Day and Labor Day weekend. The boys and I enjoy fishing, so we would try to find a campground with a good fishing hole. But we always went in an old tent camper we pulled behind the car. My idea of fun does not include sleeping on the ground!

The old camper died one spring, but we didn't want to give up our tradition. Reluctantly, I agreed to borrow a tent from a friend, and we went camping anyway. It rained the whole first night, and the tent leaked like a sieve!

We woke up the next morning in a big pool of water that had collected in our tent during the night. The rain continued the entire next day. Somehow, this weekend didn't seem so much fun anymore. By late afternoon, we gave up and went home. It was the first and last time we ever went tent camping. But we still laugh about it whenever we think about camping. It's quite a family memory.

There are some other great family benefits when we have fun together: the growing bonds of love nurtured by time spent together; heightened self-esteem for our children; the lessons we teach our children and they teach us. These are the results when we give our children and spouses our undivided attention, wholeheartedly throwing ourselves into having fun with them. So put aside those thoughts of work tomorrow, forget the clock for a few minutes, and just relax and have fun together.

The Family That Plays Together...

Those who have studied strong, happy families all agree on one thing: those families look for ways to have fun together.[8] As families enjoy each other, they are bound closer together in love and commitment to each other. To paraphrase the old slogan, "The family that plays together, stays together," and enjoys staying together a whole lot more!

These are families just like yours and mine. Some are two-parent families with both parents working outside the home. Some are single-parent families. Time is a premium for all of them. So how do they do it? How do they find time to have fun together? Let's look at a few "do's and don'ts."

- *Don't Be Afraid to Have Fun.* It may come as a surprise, but the biggest obstacle to having fun as a family is fear. We're afraid that, like Boswell's father, we'll waste our time, our money, or our energy and come up empty. But if you're convinced that having fun as a family is important and you want to try it, then banish those fears!

  And don't be afraid to put aside your work from time to time to have fun with your family. Try not to feel guilty about it. You really are doing something import-ant when you play with your family.

  Don't make the mistake of turning your play into work. Some of us, especially those who are by person-ality more intense, tend to work hard even when we play. Remember the object of family fun time is plea-sure, fun, enjoyment, and relaxation. So let go and just have fun.

- *Don't Be Afraid of the Expense.* Every fun time doesn't have to be expensive. Some special times may be, but fun is possible at all income levels. It may just require a bit more creativity. Table games or ball games in the backyard, a hike around the neighborhood, reading together, or a drive to the ice cream store may not be terribly expensive, but they can be a lot of fun.

  Family fun can be easy on the budget *and* require little planning. Younger children, for example, may enjoy a brief trip to the local museum or planetarium. When our boys were young, it seems as if we went to the local city museum about once a month. The big attraction was the dinosaur exhibit. On a rainy Saturday when the house suddenly felt too small or when we just needed some quick and inexpensive fun, someone would say,

"Let's go see the dinosaurs." Of course, there was usually time for a visit to the stuffed animals in the nature exhibit and a visit to the American History room. On the average, our visits didn't last more than an hour (young bodies tire quickly), but it was a very enjoyable hour just the same.

If you happen to live in or near a city with neighborhood parks, a weekend family picnic makes a fun outing. Some parks have nature trails for exploring or hiking. If your and your spouse's work schedules allow, meeting there for a picnic dinner after work could be a real treat.

When we lived in the city some years ago, our house was within a couple of miles of both the local Boys Club and a neighborhood school. Each had an indoor pool and set aside at least one evening a week for a "family swim." For a total of $6, we could swim and play around in the water for up to two hours.

- *Don't Be Afraid to Be Spontaneous.* We adults tend to suppress our spontaneity. It upsets our schedules. But children love it! Spontaneity gives their lives (and ours too) an element of adventure and surprise.

  Almost every day, small but important opportunities to drop everything and have fun present themselves. Just watch for them. When your "tight" schedule "loosens," go ahead and change direction. Break out of your routine. Don't be afraid to be spontaneous. Your children will love it.

- *Don't Be Afraid to Include the Children.* A friend of mine recalls that when he was a child his father always seemed to be busy at something, even when he was not at work. He enjoyed building and repairing things around the house and was often in his basement working on some "project."

It would have been easy for that father to give his son the impression that any question or interruption was a bother. After all, when you're busy on a project and hurrying to finish it, the most discouraging words you can hear are, "Daddy, can I help?" If you say yes, you know your project will take three times as long.

But my friend remembers that his father was never too busy to find *some* way to include his son. It's no surprise then, that some of my friend's best childhood memories are of those times when his father included him in his "busy-ness." Helping his dad work was *fun*. My guess is the same would apply to mothers and daughters (and mothers and sons).

Children love to participate in adult activities. They love to "help." Sometimes, if you just *have* to clear out the garage, do some yard work, run an errand, or clean the house, take time to include your children. The older they get, the more creative you have to be to involve them in such a way that they enjoy it (teens are often allergic to work), but the younger ones are usually eager to help. It gives them a sense of pride and acomplishment.

So don't be afraid to include your children in *any* activity they can do with you. If you can't avoid the activity, and they can be involved with you in a fun way, that's what beating the clock is all about.

- *Do Make Fun a Family Priority.* During the eighties, many adults came to realize that exercise and recreation are an important part of a healthy, balanced lifestyle. Health clubs and indoor racquetball clubs sprang up all over the country. Exercise and recreation became a priority for many.

  The nineties is the time to make family fun a priority. It's essential to a balanced, healthy *family* life. Helping our children develop healthy patterns of recreation and fun will ensure their future physical, emotional, and spiritual health.

Whether you have a "family sport" (skiing, bowling, etc.), love to play table games, enjoy the outdoors, find pleasure in reading together, or enjoy working on common projects, make family fun a priority. Let your children see you put aside your work from time to time and just have fun with them.

It's true, however, that the really important things in life—the things we count as priorities—rarely "just happen." Rather, they happen because we make them happen. So choose some ways to have fun with your family. Make it a priority. Then, make it happen.

- *Do Plan and Schedule Ahead.* Someone said that the way to determine a person's priorities is to examine his checkbook. This is based on the notion that a person spends his money on the things that are really important to him. There's a lot of truth to that. But there's another book that reveals what's important to a person: her appointment book.

Time is the currency of life, and we all have only a limited amount to spend. As we battle the clock today, time, not money, may truly be our most precious commodity. With time so precious, there's only one way to be sure we use it in pursuit of the things that are really important to us. We must plan and schedule ahead.

If we are going to have that fun time together, we have to make it a priority and schedule a time each week or blocks of time on a week-to-week basis. There's no other way to get it done!

Not all family fun times require advance planning, but they all require your availablity. Scheduling them on your calendar helps ensure you'll be available. "In our busy lifestyle, we may never find time to share rich experiences with our children. We must make time for this important aspect of parenting. We must put aside quality time and commit ourselves to keeping that time as a sacred obligation. And when we do, much of what we want our children to know about our beliefs and value system will be passed along to them effectively."[9]

So block out time for that camping trip, that visit to a nearby town you've always wanted to see, that soccer tournament, that recital, or even that loud concert your teenager wants to attend. If we never plan for these events, never make time in our schedules, they'll likely never happen.

One way that I block off time for larger, more time-consuming family activities is to mark on my calendar the weekdays and week-long periods during the school year when my children don't have school. Many of their "days off" fall on Fridays or Mondays. These provide good opportunities for "weekend getaways" or day trips.

Every June, the school system releases the schedule for the coming year. I copy it into my schedule right away. By putting these holidays in my calendar as soon as they are available, I can plan well in advance for special days and weekends when our family can take a break from our busy schedules and spend concentrated time having fun together. If someone asks me to do something else on one of those days, I can answer truthfully, "I'm sorry, but I have a prior commitment."

On a smaller scale, some parents try to schedule every Saturday morning or a certain evening each week for a "family time." In the spirit of beating the clock, a family fun time can be combined some weeks with the "family night" discussed in chapter 5.

Some parents reserve as a "sacred obligation" what they call "Our Day" or "My Day." Whatever it is called, on that special day, once a year, a parent and child spend the entire day together enjoying an activity or activities chosen by the child.[10] Anything within reason and within the family budget is allowed on "My Day." This can be the highlight of your child's year. As one parent described it: "They were either always looking forward or backward to it. It was a time near their birthday when they spent an entire day with Dad and could choose anything their hearts desired. And Dad paid the bill."[11]

I'll bet Dad looked forward to those special days too and scheduled them well in advance. For him, they must have been a very high priority, and his calendar would have reflected that.

- *Do Try to Find a Family Activity (or Two).* Our family knows from experience how much fun family camping can be. We never mastered the art of gourmet cooking over a kerosene stove, but the food always tasted special. Fishing, hiking, and just enjoying the fresh air can be true recreation and fun for all members of the family. We were able to keep expenses down by sharing a tent camper (and the costs!) with another couple.

  We also enjoy what we call "exploring." I hasten to add that does not mean anything so daunting as navigating wilderness rivers or underground caves. It usually means an hour or so drive to a nearby town or area we haven't visited before. Maybe your family doesn't enjoy outdoor sports or camping. Perhaps you and your family would enjoy visiting a local nursing home on a monthly basis or helping at the homeless shelter. For some families, these are not only service projects that strengthen and make visible their faith, but they are activities they genuinely enjoy doing together. If that's the case for you, rejoice! You've beaten the clock again.

- *Do Have Fun in Your Faith.* Do the words *faith* and *fun* sound contradictory to you? There is much about the Christian faith that is properly solemn, but there's also much to celebrate. Unfortunately, our children's most formative impressions of following Christ are those they receive in church where the mood is often sober and fun seems out of place.

Our children have a right to know that it's okay— even good!—for Christians to laugh and have fun. Our Lord is not upset when we take a necessary break from work. After all, He rested after He finished the creation. He's not upset when we do nothing more than have fun and enjoy each other. His first miracle was to change water into wine at a wedding party.[12] So look for ways to have fun within the fellowship of your church. Laugh and enjoy each other as Christians. It's good for you, and it's a great example for your children.

One Easter weekend I was invited to lead some special children's programs for a large church in the Washington, D.C., area. Generally I don't like to be away from home on that weekend, but this was an offer I couldn't refuse. On Saturday, the church sponsored a carnival from 1:00 - 5:00 P.M. There were clowns and refreshments. The church gym was lined with games: the duck pond, bean bag toss, mini-bowling, and a dozen other games children could enjoy. There was even a puppet show.

In the middle of it all, I had about forty-five minutes to talk to everyone (about one hundred children and fifty adults) on the "Good News" of Easter. Then everyone went outside for an easter egg hunt. On Sunday, I gave two more special children's programs with some contests and prizes during "children's church" time. After the two services, there was another easter egg hunt.

This was designed as a special attraction to reach

neighborhood people who came to church rarely but were likely to come on Easter. It appealed to me as a way to reinforce in the minds of the children what a special day of celebration the Resurrection is! We are a people of Resurrection faith. We have much to celebrate, and a certain amount of fun and celabration is entirely appropriate for Christians.

Weekend retreats for children or for entire families should offer opportunities for fun as well as learning, reflection, and worship. Service projects can also be valuable family fun times. Churches that facilitate family fun times do their families a great service.

Family fun really *is* serious business. It creates family memories, bonds your family closer together, and provides the "fun that refreshes" and recreates tired bodies and spirits.

A family that takes time to enjoy each other in healthy ways is much stronger as a result. And the children learn some important lessons for life. They'll learn to be healthy adults who can live life with a proper balance of work and play, seriousness and laughter. They'll learn to enjoy life to the full, as God intended. They'll learn that the really important things in life–the priorities of life–center on being with other people and enjoying and serving others as an expression of their Christian faith.

Perhaps they'll also learn to control their time rather than be controlled by it; in other words they'll learn to beat the clock. So don't neglect family fun. Take the time and make the time for it. It really *is* serious business. Enjoy it together–without guilt!

CHAPTER NINE

_____

_____

_____

Punching Out the Clock: Balancing Your Job and Your Family

In the spring of 1990, a bomb rocked the investment business. Peter Lynch, the forty-seven-year-old superstar director of the Fidelity Magellan mutual funds announced he was quitting to spend more time with his daughter.

Both Lynch's fourteen-hour workdays and the lucrative results for his investment fund were legendary among investors. Lynch loved what he was doing, he said, but came to the conclusion that the price he paid for such success wasn't worth it. He hardly knew his daughter. "I don't know anyone who wished on his deathbed that he had spent more time at the office."[1]

Lynch is just one of the more prominent examples of working parents who have chosen to "punch out" the clock so that they can achieve a more healthy balance between time spent on the job and time with their family.

Work, more than anything else, gets in the way of strong family relationships, observes Dolores Curran.[2] Data from the U.S. Census Bureau shows that parents have appreciably less time—from twelve to eighteen hours less each week—to spend with their children than they did in 1960.[3] A survey conducted by the Massachusetts Mutual Life Insurance Company shows that many of us believe that the fact that parents have less time to spend with their families is the most important cause of frustration and stress in our everyday family lives.[4] The reason for this lack of time for the family is often our heavy job commitments.

For single parents (most of whom are mothers), the stress is even heavier. The burden of dealing with a sick child, after-school day-care, or just letting in the plumber falls on one set of shoulders alone.

It would be ideal if anyone who wished could have the luxury Peter Lynch had and just quit (or at least cut back). But for many working parents (especially single parents), full-time work is an economic necessity.

Sometimes, there's more at the heart of the "family time famine"[5] (caused in part by job commitments) than just economic necessity, however. Sociologist Robert Bellah, who is also a professing Christian, recognizes that work is necessary but that "the *amount of time people work* is due to more than necessity. It is also due to the commodification of family life in light of expanding consumer goods that quickly become defined as 'needs (emphasis added)[6.]'"

Bellah's argument is that our economy is sustained by the continued development and sale of goods families come to think of as "needs," not just luxuries. So we parents are tempted to work longer hours in order to meet those "needs." The result, of course, is that we have less time available for our families.

The Idolatry of Work

Arlie Hochschild, author of *Second Shift*,[7] a book about the struggles of women in two-career families, points to an even more basic problem than the economic one:

> ... for all the talk about the importance of children, the cultural climate has become subtly less hospitable to parents who put children first. This is not because parents love children less, but because a "job culture" has expanded at the expense of a "family culture."[8]

This "job culture" defines work as the activity that gives life its greatest meaning and most significant rewards. As a result, work takes precedence over all other demands on our time, including family.[9]

Family goals are common, communal goals: having and nurturing children, caring for the elderly, and "building life's most enduring bonds of affection, nurturance, mutual support, and long-term commitment."[10] The goals of men and women caught up in the job culture are, by contrast, basically individualistic: "social recognition, wages, opportunities for advancement, and self-fulfillment."[11] Elsewhere, I have argued that this "careerism" combines with our larger American fascination with self-interest ("What's in it for me?") and independence ("I want to be me") to undermine and overwhelm the interdependence and self-sacrifice that successful family life requires.[12]

Hochschild and others have correctly observed that a large part of the reason for the much lamented "decline" of the family today is this job culture, which forces parents to choose between their jobs and their families. It tells us that there really isn't any choice; our jobs are what really matters. This is nothing less than the "idolatry of work" and should be seen for what it really is: "a sustained and vicious attack on the family."[13]

Nothing less than recognizing the priority of people over possessions, the inestimable value of children, and the worthiness of self-sacrifice for the good of the family will turn back this vicious attack. Who better to lead it than followers of Jesus Christ, the one who called children to His side and gave His life as a sacrifice for a world of people He deeply loved?

Although this idolatry of work sorely tempts families today, it is slowly changing under pressure from working parents. Many, like Peter Lynch, are simply refusing to choose between having a good job and having a strong family. They want to be freed from "a stressful, fragmented, unbalanced lifestyle" and choose to live "where work and parenting are integrated into one single 'career.'"[14]

What many working parents are demanding is a greater measure of control over their work schedules so that they can spend more time with their families. As many as eight out of ten say they would be willing to accept lower pay and slower advancement in exchange for just that.[15] But gaining any measure of control over your work schedule may not be easy. Not all companies offer choices. For single parents, unable to afford a drop in income, options such as part-time work, job sharing, or reduced hours are not viable choices.

However, for many of us there is often *some* choice. We can choose to have *some* control over our work schedules, if only in the area of flexibility.

Many of us *can* begin to "punch out the clock." We *can* achieve a greater degree of control over our work schedules. And when we do, our families will benefit. Families who keep their work commitments under control are likelier to be healthier and happier than those who let their work schedules control their family time.[16]

In a recent survey of 521 of the nation's largest corporations, over 90 percent said that they offer various kinds of alternative work schedules such as flextime, job sharing, and summers off.[17] In fact, working parents today are experimenting with a whole range of choices that enable them to have a greater degree of control over their work schedules and more time with their familes. Let's take a look at some of these choices and some of the people who are making them.

New Choices in the Workplace

When Peter Lynch announced he was quitting his high profile job to spend more time with his daughter, he set off an earthquake of publicity. All around the country working parents are making similar decisions and sending tremors throughout the workplace.

One woman in Tenafly, New Jersey, sold her executive search firm and gave up a six-figure income to work part-time and raise her children.[18] A manager of software development for IBM took parental leave when his children were born. He goes to work later now since he drops the children off at day-care three days a week. He also leaves the office promptly at five so he can pick them up, feed them, and play with them before bedtime.[19]

Chris is a father who made a similar choice. At thirty-four, he had worked for nine years for a bio-technology company in California. Before his son was born, both Chris and his wife worked long hours and many weekends searching for miracle drugs. Now, he works 9:00 A.M. to 5:45 P.M. and is home on weekends to be with his wife and son. Chris explained his motivation for a reduced work week this way: "I can't have my child in day-care for a twelve-hour day. He won't be my child. When you're all done, someone else will have raised him."

Chris took three months off during his son's first year "to get to know him better" and so that his wife could go back to work. He knows he has put his career "on hold," but he is happy with the results.[20]

Cheryl is a senior vice president for a major regional bank. She often was away from home from 7:30 A.M. to 7:00 P.M. Her son let her know she wasn't spending enough time with him. Fortunately, her bank had a "SelectTime" policy that enabled employees to reduce their working hours and still retain benefits and opportunities for advancement. She chose to work a four-day week and is very pleased that her son doesn't complain about her not spending enough time with him anymore.[21]

Vickie, who is an information systems manager for a New Jersey chemical and pharmaceutical company, worked out a variation on Cheryl's arrangement. She wanted to cut back to part-time when she became pregnant, but her boss had a better idea. Now, each week she works three days in the office and two days at home. At home, she "telecommutes" to her office, using her computer modem.[22]

Many of these arrangements would have been unheard of and unacceptable just a decade ago. Why are so many companies granting employees such flexibility and control over their work schedules? Because working parents are demanding them and companies are finding it in their best interest to respond.

Companies have seen the predictions: a labor force that is projected to grow much more slowly in the near future (at less than half the rate of the seventies). This means fewer young workers entering the labor market.[23]

So where will new employees come from? For the next decade, the Department of Labor estimates that two of every three new workers will be women.[24] They represent the largest pool of potential new employees for the remainder of this century. That fact, combined with the shrinking labor force, means that women (and reliable, productive workers of either sex) have significant bargaining power to demand changes in the workplace that will benefit family life.

Cheryl's bank says the "SelectTime" program of providing flexible and reduced hours is open only to employees who want to reduce their work hours for family reasons, not "to someone who just wants to reduce his or her hours to play tennis." And there is a real benefit to the bank's bottom line. Many of the employees who have chosen the "SelectTime" program have eight years or more experience and are at or near the vice president level. They are also beginning to start families. If they don't get flexibility, they'll switch to another company. The bank has a lot invested in them. It expects to hold on to that investment by providing them the flexibility and control over the work time they want.[25]

No Longer a "Women's Issue"

Managing the demands of home, full-time career, and personal life has produced enormous stress for many women and their families. As one woman put it, "Women see the damage all around them and are making different choices than they did a few years ago."[26]

One young assistant buyer for a California department store decided that her $30,000 salary wasn't worth the toll on her family and personal life. She quit and has no plans to return.[27] Other women and some men have cut back to part-time work or work at home (in child care, word processing, or home-based businesses) in order to spend more time with their families.

Working parents today are questioning and often rejecting the anti-family priorities fed them by the "job culture." "Clearly, there's a stirring in the hearts of many baby boomers reassessing priorities and questioning the sacrifices that are often required in terms of family life by unbridled 'careerism.'"[28]

Slowly, but perceptibly, men are making similar choices. They, too, want more time with their families. They are often less willing to relocate, work overtime, or have their performance measured simply by hours on the job.[29] Some, such as Chris in California or Peter

Lynch in New York, are simply doing what mothers have always done: re-arranging career priorities and trading off pay, security, and status to find time to be with their children."[30]

Others are taking responsibility for caring for their children in addition to their paid employment. Alvin is a probation officer in Detroit and father to two young girls. In his house, he's the one who "makes breakfast, gets the kids off to school, stays with them when they're sick, and bakes cakes and cookies." Alvin is one of a new and still rare breed of husband who is trying to share responsibility for parenting and housework with his wife.[31]

Single dads are even rarer, and they often have to have a good sense of humor to keep going in the face of financial constraints, just like single mothers. When one single father was asked, "Do you have a housekeeper?" he replied "No, we buy food first."[32]

Thanks to this new breed of fathers who also want to balance work and family life, the problem of how to maintain a balance between the two is no longer just a "women's issue." It's now a "parental issue." Solving it is no longer primarily a "woman's responsibility." It's now a "parental responsibility."

Many companies, including some of the nation's largest—IBM, AT&T, and others—recognize the necessity of building a "family-friendly" workplace. They are offering working parents many new weapons in their battle to beat the clock.

Some options are clearly more "family-friendly" than others. Next, we'll evaluate some of the major policies and practices offered by companies to parents in the workplace today. We'll see which ones are the most useful tools for reaching a healthy balance between work and family time.

When Is "Family-Friendly" Not So Friendly?

Flextime, job-sharing, on-site day-care, telecommuting, emergency sick child care—these are just a few of the major "family-friendly" options offered by companies today. But some of these options are more "family-friendly" than others.

It's important to remember why companies usually offer these new options: in order to stay competitive in recruiting and retaining the best workers, especially women. But don't be fooled. It's also important to recognize that "companies are mostly interested in easing the lives of working parents so that these employees can devote more 'quality time' to the firm. For quite understandable reasons, corporate America is more interested in better workers than it is in better parents."[33]

There are some notable exceptions to this assessment. Ben and Jerry's, the gourmet ice cream manufacturer, doesn't permit it's employees to stay late at work. At 6:00 P.M., they are told to go home to their families.[34] NCNB's "SelectTime" program allows employes to reduce the number of hours they work weekly (while retaining benefits and opportunities for advancement) to spend more time with their families. "We wanted to make a statement that we respect family responsibilities," a bank official said.[35]

But while these are notable exceptions, they are exceptions, nonetheless. So in evaluating the major options companies offer to working parents, let's ask two questions. The first is: "Does this option help me spend more time with my family, or is it just tempting me to spend more time on the job?"

The second question is: "Is this option in the best interests of my child (or children)?"

It is important to answer both of these questions when evaluating the new choices offered to working parents today. If the answer to both is yes, it really is a "family-friendly" option. It really will help working parents "punch out the clock" and balance their work and family time.

Job Sharing and Part-Time Work

Gretchen faced a dilemma. When her daughter was two and a half, she went back to work from 8:00 A.M. to noon daily at Kodak in Rochester. But soon it became clear that her job required full-time attention. Because Kodak permits various kinds of alternative work schedules, Gretchen was able to resolve her dilemma. She found another working mother, Barbara, who also wanted to cut back to a part-time schedule. Now the two women share one full-time job. Gretchen works all day Monday through Wednesday and Barbara works all day Wednesday through Friday.

This job-sharing arrangement allows Babrbara to go to story hour with her three-and-a-half-year-old once a week and get her grocery shopping and errands done so she can be available to her family on weekends. She also has time to be involved with her church.

Gretchen appreciates the extra time with her young daughter on those mornings when she doesn't go to work. There's another benefit: "On the days I'm off, my daughter and I visit an elderly woman I feel very close to. We take her to lunch or visit her at home. The time with her is important and I'd never be able to fit it in if I worked five days."[36]

Job-sharing is a popular and growing option for many working parents. Sometimes, when job-sharing is not available, an alternative is part-time work. Mats and his wife, Mary, both work part-time (four days a week) for Honeywell in Bloomington, Minnesota. Like many two-career couples, they see part-time work as one way "to squeeze out time for their children, themselves, and each other."[37]

Ken and Gail Heffner, who are raising their children in Pittsburgh, committed themselves to permanent part-time work as soon as their children were born. Each parent works fifteen to twenty-five hours per week so that they can care for their young children themselves and have ample time to spend with them. In spite of the career and financial sacrifices they are making, they intend to continue part-time work until their children are college age.[38]

There are some drawbacks to these options of course. Job-sharing or part-time work entails some financial and career sacrifices. The pay is often lower, the benefits reduced or non-existent, and opportunities for advancement severely curtailed. Pam's situation is a good example.

Pam is vice president of a major commercial bank in New York City. Unlike most of her colleagues, she leaves work every day at 3:00 P.M. She willingly chose part-time work—and a pay cut—so that she could spend more time with her daughter. She won't quit, she says, but she does get discouraged. Each year, she gets only a token raise, makes 50 percent less than her colleagues (though she turns out almost as much work), and forgoes as much as a $30,000 annual bonus.[39]

Pam knows that she has been put on a career track for "part-timers." It's been called "the Mommy Track." It's the price they (and the few men who've tried it) pay for wanting to balance job and family. Here is the job culture at its worst. Companies offer a clear path to the top for parents who put career first and a "Mommy Track" of flexible schedules, part-time work, and job-sharing for those who want time with their families.

Like Pam, these parents are taken off the "fast track" and often must accept a lower rate of pay and expect to be passed over for promotions and raises, not because of the quality of their work, but because they've chosen to balance work and family.[40] However, "strengthening family life in the nineties cannot and should not mean the repeal of the past thirty years of new opportunities for women in the workplace and public life."[41]

Nor should it mean a new discrimination against men. As some men have already discovered, however, a similar "Daddy Track" is emerging for men who no longer agree to endless long days, weekend work, and weeks away from home.

A "Parent Track" in the workplace is ultimately very short-sighted. In the long run, it undermines efforts to maintain a productive work force.

A growing and healthy future work force depends on parents who have time to enjoy their children, raise them, and nurture them in the values of responsibility and work. It depends on future workers who grow up with a sense of self-esteem and personal responsibility: in other words, children who receive significant parental time.

Parents whose priorities include adequate time with their families prove themselves every day to be some of industry's most reliable and productive workers. This is especially true in the case of working mothers, upon whom industry will depend more and more in the coming decade. If industry does not help working parents achieve a healthy balance between work and family without penalizing them, it will demoralize and lose many of its best employees.

If job-sharing and part-time work can be separated from the "Parent Track," they can be very positive choices for working parents. In fact, "for many dual worker households, which today account for 24.9 million children, job sharing would seem to be the ultimate win-win situation. The working parent is able to achieve real balance in his or her life. The company retains highly productive employees who might otherwise be forced to leave. The child gets to see more of Mom and Dad." [42]

There are a lot of kinks to be worked out before job-sharing and part-time work reach their full potential as "family-friendly" choices for working parents. Real and clear career paths to the top for both women and men need to be developed. And for single parents, it may be a long time before either of these options pay enough to be a viable choice.

But even with their present limitations, these are two "family-friendly" choices. They do free working parents to spend more time with their children, and that is clearly good for both parent and child. Everyone wins—except the clock.

Flextime

Flextime is another popular option offered by many companies today. Flextime usually means carrying a full-time workload during non-traditional working hours, such as 6:30 A.M. to 2:30 P.M.

A recent survey of 521 large companies around the country found that 50 percent offered flextime.[43] For example, at Hewlett-Packard, a California-based computer and electronics company, all employees can work flexible hours with the agreement of their supervisor. The only stipulations are that they work no less than eight hours and begin work between 6:00 and 8:30 A.M.[44]

Flextime may not free up any more time for working parents to spend with their children, but it allows parents to spend more "prime time" daylight hours with their children without the financial sacrifices of part-time work. Dr. Kyle Pruett, Clinical Professor of Psychiatry at the Yale University Child Study Center, feels that flextime "may, in fact, be the most valuable of all the business solutions for the child because it permits parents to plan their time for child care in ways *they* choose, not at the convenience of their employers. Such flexibility may, for example, eliminate the need for full-time day-care in some two-career families."[45] Interestingly, Pruett says that flextime "is rated by many fathers as the most desirable work-related aid to their fathering."[46]

Flextime is not for everyone. Suppose you can start work at 6:00 A.M. If you need day-care, you might have trouble finding a center open at that time of the morning. But it is a valuable option. It can offer working parents some limited flexibility in rearranging their schedules to better use the time they already have with their familes. Within limits, then, flextime is certainly "family-friendly."

Working at Home and Telecommuting

More and more working parents are looking for opportunities to work either part-time or full-time at home.

According to Dr. Kathleen Christensen, Director of the National Project on Home Based Work, more than half a million mothers of children under the age of six work at home. Most do free-lance work or run their own businesses, but some work for large companies.[47]

The total number of people who have "turned in their white or blue collars" for the "open collar" of working at home is estimated at thirty to thirty-five million.[48] The fuel that drives this trend may be the growth of the dual-career family.

While both parents may wish to work, neither necessarily wants to be out of the house and away from the family for eleven hours each day.[49] A prominent New York City business and financial writer believes that the desire of parents to "grow up with their kids, to feed the baby, or take a child to Little League" has become an "emotional imperative" for many parents today.[50] Working at home helps achieve that.

Of course, working at home takes many forms. A common job (which my wife chose while I was in seminary) is to offer family day-care. Other folks may be free-lance writers, do word processing or bookkeeping, or run a home-based business. Some are "telecommuters" who are regularly employed by a business but work at least part-time at home.

One such telecommuter is Valerie. She designs computer systems for a communications firm in Denver. Her computer terminal at home is connected directly to the company's mainframe computer. She does at least half of her work each week from her office, a converted bedroom at home.

Valerie has the benefits of being at home much of the time, having no commute, and having a flexible schedule. More important, she feels she has more time for her two pre-school children and her husband.[51]

In some cases, companies not only permit telecommuting, but encourage it. At New York Life and Pacific Bell, when an employee is allowed to telecommute from home, they receive a computer and software. This makes their home literally an extension of their office. Both of these companies and the telecommuters themselves feel this arrangement has been well worth the investment.[52]

Of course, telecommuting and working at home are not all roses. Some people miss the camaraderie of the office. Some have difficulty maintaining a disciplined schedule or meeting deadlines, especially if they have to care for young children while trying to write, type, or design. Some have trouble leaving work at the "office" when they never physically leave the "office."

Telecommuting offers working parents some of the virtues of flextime as well as some of the virtues of part-time work or job-sharing (just being able to be there and being available to our children more often and more readily). It, too, is a "family-friendly" option.

Family Leave

The first "family leave" bill was introduced in Congress in 1985. Since then, family leave has been hotly debated. Laws and practices vary from state to state and company to company, yet there is little debate over whether parental leave to care for newborns is a good thing. Most experts agree that both parents and babies need time (the exact length is still being debated) to get to know each other and "bond" together.

If that is true, then some kind of family leave ought to be the right of any working parent. Families are too important to society and to the workplace to neglect.

Any discussion of family leave immediately raises the questions "How long?" "For whom?" and "How will business survive the cost?" The Family and Medical Leave Act, first introduced in Congress in 1990 and vetoed by President Bush in 1992, was finally passed in early 1993. It requires companies of over fifty employees to provide twelve weeks of unpaid leave and continued health benefits on the occasion of childbirth, adoption, or serious family illness.

Some Christian groups, such as the Family Research Council, which began as an arm of Dr. James Dobson's Focus on the Family, opposed the bill on the grounds that it would send a signal that twelve weeks was sufficient time for parent-child bonding to take place.[53] Many business leaders opposed the bill because they felt that a mandated leave of this duration would be too costly and difficult to implement.

The latter objection—cost and difficulty—was put to rest by a recent study by the Families and Work Institute. It studied parental leave laws in four states and found "no significant increases in costs to businesses after the law went into effect, little change in the number of women taking maternity leave, and little difference in the lengths of leaves (an average of 12 weeks for women)."[54]

Although one spokesperson for a business coalition said the study showed that national legislation was clearly "an unnecessary intrusion into the workplace," that may not be the case. More fathers took leaves after the birth of a child—and their leaves were longer—only after the laws were enacted.[55]

Despite the fact that many more firms offer paternity leaves today than a decade ago, only about 1 percent of men use them. They know that if they do, they face the "wimp factor." A man taking a three-month paternity leave "is not seen as serious or committed" to his work. He's in danger of being relegated to the "Daddy Track."[56]

Legislation to mandate parental leave—even unpaid leave—might protect employees who can't negotiate their own leave and also encourage more fathers to take time to get to know their children sooner. The cost is really not a factor.[57]

Family leave is certainly a "family-friendly" option. Working parents should not be forced to choose between the needs of their children and the demands of their jobs. A generous, universal parental leave policy will eliminate one more instance where parents are forced to make that cruel choice.

Child Care Options

At the Johnson and Johnson headquarters in New Brunswick, New Jersey, there is a sleek, white building with low windows designed by internationally famous architect I.M. Pei. The building features state-of-the-art equipment, including a computer lab.

This modern building serves two hundred clients, but they are not Johnson and Johnson's usual customers. These clients range from six weeks to six years old. This is the corporate headquarters day-care center.

Johnson and Johnson takes day-care seriously. It pays the day-care staff salaries that are competitive with those of beginning public school teachers. It subsidizes two-thirds of the cost of the service in addition to the cost of the building and its maintenance. Why all this expense? The company feels it is worth the cost to be able to attract and maintain a productive workforce, especially women.[58]

At the prestigious Washington, D.C. law firm of Wilmer, Cutler, and Pickering, if you have a child-care emergency (either your child or your baby-sitter is sick), you can bring your child to the firm's emergency/sick child-care center for free. This service costs the firm $50,000 a year but the firm estimates that it saves $180,000 annually in reduced absenteeism from employees who would otherwise miss work to care for their sick children.[59]

IDS Financial Services, a subsidiary of American Express, set up a similar sick-child care center at its headquarters in Minneapolis. It's called "Chicken Soup" and caters to mildly ill children. IDS also offers an in-home emergency care service and pays 75 percent of the cost of both.[60]

Should we congratulate these and the many other companies that offer working parents this kind of child-care help? Perhaps. It is true that they *have* responded to a very real need. But are on-site day-care and sick-child care facilities the best response for families? Are they really "family-friendly"?

On the surface, on-site day-care appears to be a long overdue development. However, the dangers for children cared for by low-paid, under-educated caregivers who leave as soon as a better job comes along are well documented.[61] Johnson and Johnson's highly paid and educated staff is still the exception in the day-care industry.

British pediatrician Dr. Penelope Leach speaks for many other child development experts when she observes that, while full day-care may be a developmental plus for a three-year-old, it is not necessarily good for an infant or toddler. These younger children "need individualized care by people who know them well and are committed to their development and happiness." Whatever its advantages for employees or employers, day-care "is not designed to meet the developmental needs of babies. Infants and toddlers, who make up a large and growing segment of the day-care population, need a "parent-substitute" (often a mother who is also caring for her own child) such as is found in family day-care."[62]

On-site day-care may be good for business and helpful in relieving the stress of working parents ignore but as Dr. Pruett observed, "whether it is a better choice for the child is another question."[63] Dr.Leach put the issue squarely: "We must decide whether the day-care we provide will be the kind that employers and parents want or the kind that children need."[64]

What about sick-child care? At least from a child's perspective, when she is sick, she wants to be cared for by her parents, not a stranger. Parents know their children best, and most often, theirs is not only the most desirable but the best care a sick child can get.

According to Yale Professor and child pyschology expert Dr. Edward Ziglar, a real "pro-family" policy is one that helps parents do a better job as parents.[65] Judged by that criteria and our original ones ("Does it help me spend more time with my family?" "Is it in the best interests of my child?"), on-site child-care and sick-child care can hardly be called "family-friendly."

Instead of helping parents balance work and family time, these and some other options offered by industry may do just the opposite. Wilmer, Cutler, and Pickering's emergency/sick child care pays for itself by enabling lawyers to be "freer to work toward partnerships by logging 14-hour workdays.... But even if the center has a cute name and is described as a 'family support,' is it actually good for the children who now spend even less time with their parents?"[66]

Such options, designed to free us to spend more, not less time and energy at work,[67] are neither "family-friendly" nor pro-child. A real "family-friendly" policy would be one that enables working parents to take as much responsibility for caring for their children—in sickness and in health—as they want. That is what policies such as job-sharing, part-time work, flextime, telecommuting, and parental leave are designed to do.

Real Help in Keeping a Balance

There are some real "family-friendly" choices offered to working parents today, especially in the area of parental leave. Let's take a look at a few examples.

Merck and Co., a large pharmaceutical firm, permits parents to take a six-month, child-care leave for birth or illness at partial pay and benefits. Aetna, a large insurance company, offers eight weeks of paid parental leave and up to six months more of unpaid leave. This leave is available to both fathers and mothers. Aetna has also cut the number of hours each week that an employee must work to qualify for full benefits.[68] These are small steps, but they do help working parents have time to care for their children, especially during the crucial early months of life.

IBM, the corporate giant, offers its employees a three-year break from full-time employment. The leave is unpaid except for the option of part-time work in the second and third years. Health and pension benefits continue, and a job is guaranteed at the end of the three-year period. This option can be very useful in helping dual-career families assume more of the care of their children during the first three years of life.[69]

More companies are offering some sort of leave to care for a sick child, but it is mostly unpaid and the leave policies vary widely from company to company. The growth of such a leave policy is a positive development for familes, but unless the leave carries with it a substantial percentage of pay, it will be of little help to single parents. Edward Ziglar recommends a minimum six-month leave with pay at 75 percent for three months and guaranteed health benefits.[70]

Key Bank, in Albany, New York, has a policy that must sound wonderful to many working parents. They let their tellers take the summer off so they can be with their children. Pay is prorated with full benefits.

Bruce Industries, an electronic firm in Nevada, is also attuned to the school year. It recently started a pilot program that lets mothers work from 9:00 A.M. to 2:00 P.M. so they can be home when school gets out. These mothers also get school holidays and vacations off. Let's hope Bruce soon adds fathers to this program![71]

Single Parents Need Help, Too!

Some areas still need reform, especially in paid parental leave and eliminating the "parent track" for working parents who want to balance their work with time for their families. The biggest area of concern, however, is for single parents, mostly mothers, who simply can't afford to take unpaid leave to care for newborn or sick children.

Realistically, businesses may not be able to meet their special needs—at least not soon. Here, then, is an area where churches can step in and help them "punch out the clock" on behalf of their family life.

A group of churches in the Albany, New York, area where I live, is doing just this kind of thing. They have joined together to give a grant to a nonprofit organization called "Second Blessing." Second Blessing trains people (primarily women) to put on "home shows" of merchandise for home decoration. Trainees learn how to make presentations and sell. They learn scheduling, bookkeeping, and other aspects of how to run their own business. They receive a commission on their sales. Many of Second Blessing's clients are single women with young children. These women need to be at home with their children much of the time, and they need flexible hours.

These women need work and income. But some cannot afford the required initial investment in the merchandise they will later sell. The grant from this group of churches will enable some of them to get a "start-up loan" so they can make that investment and begin the journey to self-support and caring for their children.

This type of program is aptly named. It is a blessing, both to the women involved and to their children. It's just one small example of how churches can help working parents (especially single parents) beat the clock and balance work and family life.

No matter what your family structure is, no matter what your job, you already know that beating the clock to enjoy your family is always a challenge in our busy world. I hope you can see this is a challenge we can meet. In fact, you may already be winning it. So be encouraged. Keep on beating the clock. As you do, you and your family will reap great rewards.

A Final Word: Partners in Family Life Together

He is thirty-six years old and the father of two young children. After sixteen months of working fifty-hour weeks as sales manager for a major computer software firm, he was fired. The reason? He says it was because he put his family ahead of his job.

He came in early most days but wouldn't stay late after work for training and social events. Because his wife was a flight attendant who often traveled, he felt he had to be home with his children in the evening. That was the problem. "This is not a family company and never will be," he claims his boss told him. "It's a disadvantage to be married . . . to have any other priority but work." So he was fired, and now he's suing his employer.[1]

It's not easy being a husband and a father today. Just when you think you understand what is required, the rules change. Not too long ago, a good husband and father was a "good provider" and "faithful" to his wife. Now, you need to be a good companion, communicate your feelings, be skilled in sharing the household chores, and become a full partner in parenting your children.

All the changes in our understanding of sex roles have had at least one good effect: women aren't the only ones who have been liberated; we men have been liberated too. We've been freed from the restricting and restricted role of "breadwinner/disciplinarian" to become full partners with our wives in all aspects of family life, especially the nurture of our children.

For the many men who are trying on this new role as a full partner in family life, it's a case of "Try it, you'll like it." Once they try it, they find they like it very much. A town supervisor in a suburb of Albany, New York, recently announced that he would not seek reelection so that he could spend more time with his twin toddlers. He'll still practice law, but his office will be in his home, near his children.[2]

Nearby, another man, now in his late forties, closed his thriving bookstore to become a full-time, stay-at-home parent to his sons, two and nine years old. He said he regretted not being able to spend more time with his older son earlier and didn't want to make the same mistake with his two-year-old.[3] His wife is the full-time family "breadwinner."

While all men need not be full-time, stay-at-home parents, still they must be encouraged to be a full partner in nurturing and shaping the lives of their children. Surely that is one of the special rewards of being human that we men too often miss.[4]

Many of us men can thank women for helping us learn to enjoy these rewards. And, in the past three decades, as women have taken their place beside men in the workplace, they've rediscovered what we are just learning: "that work, productivity, and marriage may be very important parts of life but they are not its whole cloth. The rest of the fabric is made of nurturing relationships, especially those with children—relationships which are intimate, trusting, humane, complex, and full of care."[5]

Today, men who truly want to be a nurturing force within their families and are acting on that desire are "a growing sociological phenomenon."[6] They have seen their chance to beat the clock on behalf of their family life, and they've decided to seize it. These men are pioneers who are redefining for the generations to come the role of husband and father as a full partner in family life.

What does it mean for a man to be a "full partner" in family life with his spouse? From the example of the men who are doing it today, we can glean these three aspects: full partnership in housework, full partnership in balancing job and family, and full partnership in nurturing children (and family life as a whole).

Partnership in Housework

Many wives are contributing twenty-five percent or more of the family income today. They have relieved many men of the burden of being the sole family "breadwinner." But have men helped relieve their wives of the burden of being the sole family "domestic engineer"?

Studies estimate that married men do thirty percent of the housework today, as opposed to twenty percent in 1965.[7] They are clearly more involved than their fathers were. But before we get too pleased with our progress, it's important to note that there's a real difference between "doing" and "being responsible." Fathers are doing more than ever, it's true, "but they are still functioning as people who 'help out.'"[8] We've still got a ways to go to reach full partnership!

Of course, couples who favor a more traditional "breadwinner/homemaker" arrangement ought to be just as free to do so—and just as honored—as any other. But those of us with wives who spend as much time in the marketplace every day as we do have an opportunity to do what is right and good at the same time: assume full partnership with our wives in household chores.

Partnership in Balancing Job and Family

Women are still carrying the larger share of the burden of balancing job and career. They are the ones who have forced employers to offer many of the new workplace choices: job sharing, part-time work, parental leave, flextime, and others. For quite some time now, they have made the career sacrifice of getting off the "fast track" and getting on the "Mommy Track" in order to spend more time with their families. They've led the revolution in the workplace so that they could have, and spend, more time with their children.

As we've seen, men are beginning to join that revolution. We're cutting back hours at work, staying home more on weekends, minimizing trips away from home, and risking the "Daddy Track" by asking for paternity leave. But there's still a lot more we can do if we're really serious about being full partners with our wives in balancing job and family.

We can start by *intentionally* risking the "Daddy Track" at work. If the best of industry's male employees join with the best women employees in demanding a truly family-friendly workplace, such a workplace will emerge much more quickly. In fact, a real "Parent Track" that enables working parents to maintain a healthy work-family balance, without discrimination in regard to promotions, salaries, and benefits, could become a reality.

The truly family-friendly workplace will only emerge when *both* men and women workers demand it. That will mean a literal revolution in the workplace and the job culture that defines it.

We men need to discover "a fundamentally new scheme for a man's life and especially the use of his time—a scheme that enhances the quality of life more than it centers on work."[9] Assuming full partnership with our wives in the nurture of our children and every aspect of our family's life is the best possible basis for that revolutionary new scheme.

In fact that revolution has already begun, and it's a revolution that can be won. When that day comes, all families will have some new and powerful tools with which to beat the clock. Single mothers and their families may benefit the most, but all families will be winners.

Partnership in Nurturing Our Children

Ask any mother who has just spent a rainy Saturday with three kids—or even a sunny day with two pre-schoolers. Being a parent is hard work. It's physically demanding and emotionally draining. That's because children need their parents: to be there, to comfort, to care, to be interested, to stimulate, to nurture, to teach and model, and so many other things. It's a big job. Maybe that's why, in the ideal scheme of things, God gave children two parents.

No one disputes the heroics of single mothers. No one can deny the healthy, happy children they raise. But it's such a struggle sometimes—for both mother and children. It can be (and ought to be) easier and—dare we say it—better, when the father is there to fully share the parenting and nurture.

In past generations, fathers have often been there physically but absent emotionally. When they are too much absent either way, both they and their children are the losers. "There's no question that when a father's relationship with his children is warm, children grow up secure, not only in the world, but in themselves."[10] Either physical or emotional absence can undermine a child's sense of self and lead to emotional and behavioral problems that can last a lifetime.[11]

Dr. Kyle Pruett, author of *The Nurturing Father: Journey Toward the Complete Man,* says that fatherhood is "the single most creative, complicated, fulfilling, frustrating, engrossing, enriching, depleting endeavor of a man's adult life."[12] It's also a great privilege. As fathers, we are partners with God and our spouses in bringing a new life to physical, emotional, and spiritual maturity. We are given the awesome gift and responsibility of nurturing an eternal spirit. For the early years, at least, we literally model God for our children.

If all that sounds a bit daunting, let me hasten to add one adjective to Dr. Pruett's list: enjoyable. Fatherhood is enjoyable, too! Enjoying our children is one of the great rewards of parenting. We were meant to enjoy our children, to delight in them, just as God, our father, delights in us. And we ought to enjoy our children for another reason—because being a good father *is* hard work.

Being a good father may mean providing material necessities, but it is so much more. It means "providing an environment of values, strength, approval, and support,"[13] as well as being a model of faith for our children to follow. We are disciples of Jesus Christ who, with our wives, disciple our children.

Who could do all this merely out of a sense of duty? Shouldn't such hard work have its rewards? Aren't we much more likely to succeed if we really enjoy our children?

Men who assume full partnership with their wives in nurturing their children and families will reap great rewards, but they must also be prepared to practice some self-discipline and sacrifice. That's not always easy. But armed with a clear sense of their priorities, they will do what is required. They will understand the wisdom in these words of Dr. James Dobson:

> I have concluded that the accumulation of wealth, even if I could achieve it, is an insufficient reason for living. When I reach the end of my days, a moment or two from now, I must look backward on something more meaningful than the pursuit of houses and land and machines and stocks and bonds. Nor is fame of any lasting benefit. I will consider my earthly existence to have been wasted unless I can recall a loving family, a consistent investment in the lives of people, and an earnest attempt to serve the God who made me. Nothing else makes much sense, and certainly nothing else is worthy of my agitation.[14]

When we fathers are armed with this credo, we, too, will have learned the true secret to beating the clock and richly enjoying our families.

SOURCE NOTES

Introduction: Unlocking the Secret

1. University of Maryland Professor John Robinson, quoted in Michelle Osborn, "Many Choose to Stay Home with Children," *USA Today*, 10 May 1991, B-2.

2. Nick Stinnett and John DeFrain, *Secrets of Strong Families* (New York: Berkeley Books, 1986), 83.

3. Ephesians 5:15-16 (NIV).

Chapter 1

1. Nancy Gibbs, "How America Has Run Out of Time," *Time*, 24 April 1989, 58.

2. Ibid., 67.

3. Ibid., 58.

4. Dolores Curran, *Stress and the Healthy Family* (Minneapolis, Minn.: Winston Press, 1985), 158.

5. Ibid., 16-20.

6. David and Barbara Bjorklund, "Happy Parents, Happy Kids," *Parents*, January 1989, 128.

7. Armand M. Nicholi, Jr., "Commitment to Family" in *Family Building: Six Qualities of a Strong Family*, ed. George Rekers (Ventura, Calif.: Regal Books, 1985), 53.

8. Dennis B. Guernsey, *The Family Covenant: Love and Forgiveness in the Christian Home* (Elgin, Ill.: David C. Cook, 1984), 61.

9. Royce Money, *Building Stronger Families* (Wheaton, Ill.: Victor Books, 1984), 40.

10. "Unmarried Parents Look for Support," Albany *Times-Union*, 11 October 1988, A-1.

11. Jane Blotzer, "The Feminization of Poverty," *Pittsburgh Post-Gazette*, 13 October 1986, 9.

12. The Family: Preserving America's Future, The Report of the White House Working Group on the Family, Nov. 1986, 26.

13. Quoted in Gibbs, "How America Has Run Out of Time," 61.

14. Richard Patterson, Jr., *Brand-Name Kids: The Loss of Childhood in America* (Old Tappan, N.J.: Revell, 1988), 124-5.

15. Christopher Lasch, *Haven in a Heartless World* (New York: Basic Books, 1977), xv, xvii.

16. Quoted in Gibbs, "How America Has Run Out of Time," 58.

17. Patterson, 143-58.

18. Quoted in Gibbs, "How America Has Run Out of Time," 67.

19. Stinnett and DeFrain, *Secrets of Strong Families*, 30.

Chapter 2

1. Louise Tutelian, "Hello, Could I Speak with My Mom, Please?," *Working Mother*, May 1989, 61-2.

2. Deuteronomy 6:1-9.

3. Dolores Curran, *Traits of a Healthy Family*, (Minneapolis, Minn.: Winston Press, 1983), 56.

4. Ibid.

5. First Corinthians 12:20-22.

6. Matthew 22 and Luke 14:15ff.

6. Carol Luebering, "Reclaiming the Family Meal," *Marriage and Family*, March 1990, 22.

8. Ibid., 23.

9. Stinnett and DeFrain, *Secrets of Strong Families*, 96-97.

Chapter 3

1. Stinnett and DeFrain, *Secrets of Strong Families*, 83

2. Paul Stephens, *Marriage Spirituality* (Downers Grove, Ill.: InterVarsity, 1989), 55.

3. "When Workers Worry about Their Children," *Albany Times-Union*, 30 May 1990, C-12.

4. Quoted in Ibid.

5. Quoted in Ibid.

6. Louise Tutelian, "Hello, Could I Speak with My Mom, Please?," *Working Mother*, May 1989, 58.

7. Ibid., 62.

Chapter 4

1. "What Is Happiness? A Great Marriage," Interview with Dr. Joanna Magda Polenz in *USA Today*, 14 Feb. 1990, 11A.

2. O. R. Johnson, *Who Needs the Family?* (Downers Grove, Ill.: InterVarsity, 1979), 58-59.

3. Ibid., 57.

4. William P. Roberts, "Stumbling Blocks to Marital Intimacy," *Marriage and Family*, July 1990, 12.

5. David Mace, "Marriage Matters: Two Kinds of Love in Marriage," *Marriage and Family Living*, June 1988, 31.

6. Stinnett and DeFrain, *Secrets of Strong Families*, 94-95.

7. Tim Stafford, "Intimacy: Our Latest Sexual Fantasy," *Christianity Today*, 16 Jan. 1987, 22.

8. Johnson, *Who Needs the Family?*, 60.

9. Stinnett and DeFrain, *Secrets of Strong Families*.

10. Ibid., 83.

11. Johnson, *Who Needs the Family?*, 57.

12. Sondra Forsyth Enos, "20 Warning Signs of a Marriage Heading for Trouble," *Working Mother*, August 1989, 17.

13. Johnson, *Who Needs the Family?*, 57.

14. Enos, "20 Warning Signs," 19.

15. Paul Stephens, *Marriage Spirituality*, 40.

16. Ibid., 44.

17. Quoted in *Leadership*, Spring 1990, 48.

18. Stephens, *Marriage Spirituality*, 19.

19. Johnson, *Who Needs the Family?*, 60.

20. I borrowed this very useful illustration from Stinnett and DeFrain, *Secrets of Strong Families*, 49.

21. Quoted in "Maples: No Homewrecker," Albany *Times-Union*, 20 April 1990, A-2.

22. Stephens, *Marriage Spirituality*, 56.

23. Debra Evans, "Romancing for Life: 100 Great Dates for Parents in Love," *Christian Parenting Today*, Jan./Feb., 1990, 45.

24. Ibid., 44.

25. Enos, "20 Warning Signs," 17.

26. Evans, "Romancing for Life," 46-48, 50.

27. "What Is Happiness?," 11A.

28. See Money, *Building Stronger Families*, 66-7, and Stinnett and DeFrain, *Secrets of Strong Families*, 101-2.

29. Stinnett and DeFrain, *Secrets of Strong Families*, 102.

30. Stephens, *Marriage Spirituality*, 59.

Chapter 5

1. Charles M. Sell, *Family Ministry: The Enrichment of Family Life Through the Church*, (Grand Rapids, Mich.: Zondervan, 1981), 219.

2. Deuteronomy 6:1-3.

3. Deuteronomy 6:6-9.

4. Richard D. Dobbins, "Nurturing a Healthy View of God," *Christian Parenting Today*, July/August 1989, 47.

5. Erik Erikson, *Young Man Luther* (New York: W.W. Norton, 1958), 222. See also my extensive discussion of this in *Brand-Name Kids*, 85-86, 122-23, 222.

6. Acts 20:20.

7. Johnston, *Who Needs the Family?* 36.

8. Second Timothy 1:5, 3:14-15.

9. David R. Veerman, *Serious Fun* and *More Serious Fun* (Wheaton, Ill: Victor Books).

10. David R. Veerman, "Getting Your Family into the Word," *Christian Parenting Today*, Nov./Dec., 1990, 48. I have relied on Veerman's helpful article throughout this section.

11. Dobbins, "Nurturing A Healthy View of God," 47.

12. Robert E. Webber, *The Book of Family Prayer* (Nashville, Tenn.: Thomas Nelson, 1986), 20.

13. Dean and Grace Merrill, *Together At Home: 100 Proven Ways to Nurture Your Child's Faith* (Nashville, Tenn.: Thomas Nelson, 1985).

Chapter 6

1. Deuteronomy 6:5–6, (emphasis mine).

2. Deuteronomy 6:7.

3. Money, *Building Stronger Families*, 40.

4. Kevin M. Ranaghan, "Let the Children Come to Me . . .," *New Heaven/New Earth*, November 1990, 16.

5. Ibid.

6. Ibid.

7. Ibid.

8. Deuteronomy 6:8-9.

9. Ranaghan, "Let the Children Come to Me . . .," 15.

10. Ibid, 16.

11. Psalm 34:8.

Chapter 7

1. Paul Pearsall, *The Power of the Family: Strength, Comfort and Healing* (New York: Doubleday, 1990), 38.

2. Ibid.

3. Ibid., 38-9.

4. Ibid., 39.

5. Dr. Thomas Boyce, pediatrician and researcher, quoted in Pearsall, *Power of the Family*, 42.

6. Pearsall, *Power of the Family*, 39.

7. Curran, *Traits of a Healthy Family*, 212.

8. Ibid., 210.

9. Dr. Steven Zeitlin, director of City Lore: The New York Center for Urban Folk Culture, quoted in Dena K. Salmon, "The Comfort and Joy of Family Rituals," 50.

10. Pearsall, *Power of the Family*, 44.

11. Ibid., 44-5.

12. Nancy Rubin, "Family Rituals," *Parents*, March 1989, 108.

13. Matthew 25:40 (NKJV).

14. Curran, *Traits*, 200.

15. Ibid., 206.

16. Clem Waters, "Family Traditions Form Family Ties," *New Heaven/New Earth*, November 1990, 7.

17. Dr. Evan Imber-Black, quoted in Louise Lague, "Holiday Magic," *Parents*, December 1990, 80.

18. Pearsall, *Power of the Family*, 55.

19. Curran, *Traits*, 160.

20. Waters, "Family Traditions Form Family Ties," 6.

21. Curran, *Traits*, 220.

22. Lague, "Holiday Magic," 83.

23. Susan Abel Lieberman, *New Traditions: Redefining Celebrations for Today's Family* (New York: Farrar, Strauss & Giroux, 1991).

24. Ibid., 56-7.

25. Ibid., 59.

26. Jean Grasso Fitzpatrick, "Getting Closer," *Working Mother*, December 1989, 101.

27. Waters, "Family Traditions Form Family Ties," 6.

28. Lieberman, *New Traditions*, 121-2.

29. Ibid., 125-6.

30. Ibid., 128-9.

31. Curran, *Traits*, 211.

Chapter 8

1. Quoted in "To Illustrate," *Leadership*, Spring 1989, 48.

2. Curran, *Traits of a Healthy Family*, 125.

3. Richard A. Gardner, *Understanding Children: A Parent's Guide to Child Rearing* (Cresskill, N.J.: Creative Therapeutics, 1979), 93.

4. Bruno Bettleheim, "The Importance of Play," *The Atlantic Monthly*, March 1987, 36.

5. Richard Patterson, Jr., *Brand-Name Kids: The Loss of Childhood in America* (Old Tappan, N.J.: Revell, 1988).

6. David Elkind, *The Hurried Child* (Reading, Mass.: Addison-Wesley, 1981), 159.

7. Gwen Weising, *Raising Kids on Purpose for the Fun of It* (Old Tappan, N.J.: Revell, 1989), 134.

8. Curran, *Traits*, 117, and Nick Stinnett in Jim Larson, *Growing a Healthy Family* (Minneapolis, Minn.: Augsburg, 1986), 29-30.

9. Weising, *Raising Kids*, 18.

10. Curran, *Traits*, 160.

11. Weising, *Raising Kids*, 134.

12. Genesis 2:2-3, John 2:1-11.

Chapter 9

1. Quoted in, Janice Castro, "The Simple Life," *Time*, 8 April 1991, 62.

2. Curran, *Traits of a Healthy Family*, 134.

3. Victor R. Fuchs, "Are Americans Underinvesting in Children?," in *Rebuilding the Nest: A New Commitment to the American Family*, ed. David Blankenhorn, Steven Bayme, and Jean Bethke Elshtain (Milwaukee, Wis.: Family Services America, 1990), 66.

4. Sylvia Anne Hewlett, "Good News? The Private Sector and Win-Win Scenarios," in *Rebuilding the Nest*, 216.

5. "Family Time Famine," in *Washington Watch* (published by the Family Research Council, a division of Focus on the Family), 1991, 1.

6. Robert N. Bellah, "The Invasion of the Money World," in *Rebuilding the Nest*, 231.

7. Arlie Hochschild, *Second Shift: Working Parents and the Revolution at Home* (New York, NY: Viking, 1989).

8. Hochschild, *Second Shift*, quoted in Bellah, "The Invasion of the Money World," 231.

9. See my discussion of the attitudes toward work, especially among men, in *Brand-Name Kids*, 152-58.

10. David Blankenhorn, "American Family Dilemmas," in *Rebuilding the Nest*, 12.

11. Ibid., 10.

12. See *Brand-Name Kids*, 28, 121-28.

13. Brian Knowles, "Job vs. Family: Striking a Balance," *Focus on the Family*, June 1991, 4.

14. Patterson, *Brand-Name Kids*, 155.

15. Betty Holcomb, "The Benefit of the Hour," *Working Mother*, July 1991, 34.

16. Curran, *Traits of a Healthy Family*, 139.

17. Holcomb, "The Benefit of the Hour," 32.

18. Michelle Osborn, "Many Choose to Stay Home with Children," *USA Today*, 10 May 1991, B-1.

19. Nanci Hellmich, "Many Fathers Seek Ways to Have It All," *USA Today*, 15 June 1990, D-1, 2.

20. Jim Schacter, "Leaving the Rat Race to Hop on the Dad Track," *Pittsburgh Press*, 22 October 1989, F-1.

21. Holcomb, "The Benefit of the Hour," 31.

22. Ibid., 32.

23. Hewlett, "Good News? The Private Sector and Win-Win Scenarios," 207.

24. Susan Mernit, "The Newest in Family Friendly Benefits," *Working Mother*, June 1989, 64.

25. Holcomb, "The Benefit of the Hour," 32.

26. Castro, "The Simple Life," 62.

27. Osborn, "Many Choose to Stay Home with Children," B-1.

28. Ibid., B-2.

29. Randolph E. Schmidt, "Tug of War for Working Fathers," Albany *Times-Union*, 16 June 1989, A-1.

30. Betty Holcomb, "Is the Mommy Track a Trap?," *Working Mother*, July 1989, 89.

31. Eric Larsen, "The New Father," *Parents*, June 1991, 93.

32. Sue Anne Pressley, "When Dads Are Thrust into Double Duty," *Washington Post*, 18 June 1989, D-7.

33. Hewlett, "Good News? The Private Sector and Win-Win Scenarios," 215-16.

34. Susan Seliger, "Champions of Child Care," *Working Mother*, June 1991, 60.

35. Quoted in Holcomb, "The Benefit of the Hour," 31-32.

36. Quoted in James A. Levine, "How Employees Are Helping Working Moms," *Good Housekeeping*, September 1990, 194.

37. Nanci Hellmich, "Part-time Work Promotes Full Life," *USA Today*, 16 April 1990, D-2.

38. Patterson, *Brand-Name Kids*, 150-52.

39. Holcomb, "Is the Mommy Track a Trap?," 88.

40. Ibid., 87-8.

41. Blankenhorn, "American Family Dilemmas," in *Rebuilding the Nest*, 19.

42. Hewlett, "Good News? The Private Sector and Win-Win Scenarios," 215.

43. Amy Saltzman, "The Hex of Flex," *U.S. News and World Report*, 26 Feb. 1990, 56.

44. Mernit, "The Newest in Family Friendly Benefits," 68.

45. Kyle D. Pruett, *The Nurturing Father: Journey toward the Complete Man* (New York: Warner Books, 1987), 296-97.

46. Ibid.

47. Pamela Redmond Satran, "The No Commute Career," *Child*, September 1990, 76.

48. Kate Stone Lombardi, "Business As Unusual," *Parenting*, October 1990, 86.

49. Ibid., 88.

50. Roxanne Farmanfarmaian, "Worksteading: The New Lifestyle Frontier," *Psychology Today*, November 1989, 42.

51. Levine, "How Employers Are Helping Working Moms," 194.

52. Farmanfarmaian, "Worksteading: The New Lifestyle Frontier," 46.

53. "Family Leave Policy Stirs Pro Family Feud," *Christianity Today*, 27 May 1991, 44.

54. Julia Lawlor, "Study Backs Family Leave," *USA Today*, 23 May 1991, B-6.

55. Ibid.

56. Julia Lawlor, "Men Seeking More Family Time Face 'Wimp Factor,'" *USA Today*, 14 June 1991, B-1.

57. Lawlor, "Study Backs Family Leave," B-6.

58. Seliger, "Champions of Child Care," 56.

59. Mernit, "The Newest in Family Friendly Benefits," 66-67.

60. Levine, "How Employers Are Helping Working Moms," 192.

61. For example, see Penelope Leach, "Day Care Centers Are Fine for Pre-Schoolers but What about Babies?," *Parenting*, June-July 1991, 63, and Patterson, *Brand-Name Kids*, chapter 4: "The Dilemma of Day Care."

62. Leach, "Day Care Centers Are Fine for Pre-Schoolers but What about Babies?," 60-61.

63. Pruett, *The Nurturing Father*, 296.

64. Leach, "Day Care Centers Are Fine for Pre-Schoolers but What about Babies?," 60.

65. Edward F. Ziglar and Elizabeth P. Gilman, "An Agenda for the '90's: Supporting Families," in *Rebuilding the Nest*, 245.

66. Hewlett, "Good News? The Private Sector and Win-Win Scenarios," 216.

67. Ibid.

68. Vivian Cadder, "The Best Companies for Working Mothers," *Working Mother*, October 1989, 76.

69. Ibid.

70. Ziglar and Gilman, "An Agenda for the '90's: Supporting Families," 246.

71. Seliger, "Champions of Child Care," 60.

A Final Word

1. Julia Lawlor, "Suit Puts Spotlight on 'Daddy Stress,'" *USA Today*, 21 June 1991, B-1.

2. Catherine Clabby, "Dads Enjoying Home Roles," *Albany Times-Union*, 10 June 1991, G-5.

3. Ibid.

4. Ibid.

5. Pruett, *The Nurturing Father: Journey toward the Complete Man*, 280.

6. Clabby, "Dads Enjoying Home Roles," G-1.

7. Karen Levine, "Are Dads Doing More?," *Parents*, June 1989, 73-74.

8. Ibid., 74.

9. Pruett, *The Nurturing Father*, 283.

10. Quoted in Carla Cantor, "The Father Factor," *Working Mother*, June 1991, 39.

11. Ibid., 41.

12. Pruett, *The Nurturing Father*, 282.

13. Paul Lewis, "Being Dad Just for the Fun of It," *Christian Parenting Today*, Nov.-Dec. 1989, 100.

14. Quoted in Rolf Zettersten and Jim Ware, "More Views of Dr. Dobson," *Focus on the Family*, Oct. 1989, 15.